To all of those who protested outside the Municipio in August 2005

I would like to mention all of the fine tifosi who attended both eventful and mundane Torino matches with me in the Curva Maratona: Adam Bishop, Tom Bourne, Lara Mezzanotte, Anthony Massari, Alessandra Aime, Gaetano La Delfa Campione, Benjamin Furlong, Gianpiero Orlando, Luis Francisco Garcia, Mary Kay Donovan, Maria Naxaki, James Evangelides, Peter Nordenstroem and Jeff Hallman.

A special thanks in reference to the terrible summer of 2005 to the media organs that covered the Torino affair, especially the weekly *Granatissimo* magazine, www.toronews.net, the *Orgoglio Granata* television show and all of the independent websites and news agencies that followed the 'Torino affair' with passion and vigour.

To John D Taylor and Nik Howe, two esteemed colleagues and friends from *Football Italia* magazine. To Simone Davide, an ultrà granata and his fantastic Calabrese osteria. To Franco Brunetti for his help in obtaining some key photos and press tickets.

To Tiziana Caso for her patience, understanding and research assistance during the course of writing this book and a thanks to my father for introducing me to football, despite its blatant faults.

Cover image by P Bourne (La Curva Maratona, Torino v Verona, September 2004)

© 2006 by Peter Bourne. All rights reserved.

Contents

My Fede Granata	4
Play-off Revenge	7
Superga, Meroni, Ferrini	17
Cimmi & Tilli - The Men Who Killed Torino Calcio	43
Protests, marches but no cheque	55
Torino Calcio RIP	71
Traitors?	82
The men who saved the club: The Lodisti	87
The takeover battle: Cairo v Giovannone	94
The resurrection	120
The future	128

Introduction – My Fede Granata

My fede granata is not a common one. I was not born in Turin nor Grugliasco, San Mauro, San Salvario or Nichelino. I was born in Birmingham (the real one), England, and until I was 13 years old probably had no idea of who Torino were never mind the angels of Superga, Gigi Meroni or Paolino Pulici.

One night, I say one night, I now know it was the night of the 29th April 1992, I asked my father to record some football on the BBC. I don't remember what the highlights I wanted to watch were but part of the show covered the UEFA Cup Final First Leg between Torino and Ajax.

I watched the highlights the following morning and remember immediately falling in love with Torino's Bordeaux, blood coloured shirts which seemed like fine wine flowing from a bottle of Barolo when in motion. It was a calling. You usually don't choose your football team and my team forever will be Port Vale, but that night Torino became my mistress, and one like Valentino Mazzola, I'm profusely loyal to. The wife has even come to accept the mistress.

I had always been fascinated by Italy and that together with the colour of the Torino shirts ignited my interest. If that wasn't enough, the presence of Enzo Scifo the Sardinian-born Belgian in the Torino midfield, a player I had admired with during Italia '90, probably sealed the attraction.

Torino played in a packed stadium that night and I remember praying for the Granata to score the late equaliser in the first-leg against Ajax, which eventually came from the Brazilian Walter Casagrande. The second-leg was heartbreaking, the team drawing 0-0 in Amsterdam, hitting the post three times, a post Ajax keeper Stanley Menzo kissed poetically after the match, his side having won on away goals.

I'm not sure whether my sudden new romance would have blossomed without Channel 4's coverage of Italian Football headed by James

Richardson and Paul Gascoigne. After all, Gazza joining Lazio was a major catalyst for European football interest in the UK. Ironically, Biancocelsti President Gianmarco Calleri, a major player in the fall of Torino Calcio, signed Gascoigne for Lazio.

Through Channel 4's coverage, I gathered an understanding for Torino's peculiar and tragic history (it seemed my newly found mistress was an emotional sort, and not one content with 90 minutes attention on a Sunday afternoon) followed the team in Europe and in the upper echelons in the Italian game before the worst decade of the club's history. 1995-2005: The depressing years. I feel almost to blame. Before I met Torino Calcio they had played all but two years in Serie A, since when nine campaigns in Serie B.

Through my interest in Italian football, I worked for Channel 4 and Independent Magazines on the *Football Italia* and subsequently *Calcio Italia* magazine and website, took Italian lessons and eventually a job in Turin with the XX Olympic Winter Games.

Not until my time in Italy could I really appreciate the beautiful sufferance that is Torino Calcio, the unique people involved in the story of the club, the cross-section of passionate supporters, for whom the word passionate isn't a tired cliché but a severe understatement. I've learnt to hate the team whose name doesn't appear in this book, fallen in love with players I've never seen play and spent most of the summer of 2005 campaigning for a better future whilst wandering around the Piazza del Municipio, where the future of the club was played out like a Shakespearean tragedy at the Globe.

There is no team like Torino, the first team to go bankrupt after gaining promotion, a club stripped of titles, a club which has witnessed major players tragically killed, cup final defeats, a record breaking second-place league finish and most poignantly its and Italy's greatest team wiped out in an air tragedy. Supporting Torino is a faith and was a calling, and I'm glad my father taped BBC that night.

Peter Bourne

Turin, February 2006

Chapter 1 - Play-Off Revenge

I always arrive at the stadium at least an hour before kick-off. Any earlier than an hour before kick-off and the event becomes anticlimactic, any later and you miss the rush of positive energy that is the remaining fans arrive, the curva filling like a tank of water to create a burgundy ocean, the players warming up, pools of opposition fans spilling in to subject themselves to two hours of abuse and a lock-in or a carabinieri beating at the end of the match.

Then there is the club anthem, the first flares and fireworks, the expectation that the afternoon or evening could and will go any way. Arriving on the stroke of kick-off throws me off balance and the first 20 minutes of the game is a disorientating experience. Who's playing where? What's the mood in the curva? Is the person standing next to me going to annoy me for the next hour and a half?

The first sets of supporters to arrive at the stadium are the ultrà[1] groups who from the early hours of the morning are planning the chorography, mislaying cables for megaphones and speakers or unpacking boxes of t-shirts and pins to sell at negotiable prices.

The day's attendance can usually be predicted by how many people and how soon people jump on the number 72 bus from the centre of Turin to the Stadio Delle Alpi. A home match in the ice-cold misty winter against Catanzaro, and you'll see only the flat cap fan with a personalised Torino Calcio cushion.

---

[1] the ultras are the extreme groups of organised supporters responsible for the chorography, passion and atmosphere within the stadiums and often acts of violence outside. The ultrà groups at different clubs carry varying political messages, such as the left-wing groups at Livorno, the right-wing groups at Lazio. Generally the ultras stay out of trouble, but when they don't....

For a higher profile match, it will be quickly populated by wiry thin teenagers with that stench of cheap cigarettes, big bubble gum and experiencing their first erections. Most fans don't get the bus. It takes ages. The ride is at least 40 minutes from the centre of town. The few seats are so uncomfortable you can't decide whether it's more painful to sit or stand. In order to punch and validate your ticket (for the stupid few who do so), you have to face a rugby scrum before reaching the little orange box which usually doesn't work or prints the wrong date. It's full of smelly people with stale body odour, or foreign builders asleep after a day constructing one of the city's many never-ending reurbanisation projects, to people you wouldn't dare make eye contact with, to old women who assault you for the opportunity to taking one of those few, precious uncomfortable seats.

Today everyone wants to get to the game earlier and the bus from the terminus in via Bertola was already packed. For almost 60,000 tickets have been sold, from Collegno to Chivasso, Parma to Palermo. Torino supporters are not shy in their allegiance to the club but in recent years most have stopped short of buying a match ticket. Years of mismanagement, hard luck, negligence and pain have forced all but the diehard to spend their weekends elsewhere. Today is a sign that it doesn't take a manifestation or a remembrance service to bring Toro[2] fans back together. This is a football team as well as a mind-boggling, romantic, tragic and nostalgic institution.

After a two-year absence, Torino are on the verge of a return to Serie A, a league where they have spent all but eight years of their history. Tonight is the return-leg of the playoff final against Perugia, the Granata having won the away leg 2-1, so strong favourites to claim a place back in the top-flight and in the meantime, revenge. Revenge because in the summer of 1998, Perugia beat Torino in another play-off final to claim a place in the top division. In wasn't the defeat, however it may have been enough, but the nature of the loss which created what has become a bitter rivalry between the two clubs.

With two games to go before the end of that season, Torino were decimated by injuries but three points clear of Perugia in the classifica.

---

[2] Toro is the club's nickname, translating as 'Bull' in Italian. Torino are also referred to as The Granata due to their burgundy-coloured shirts.

The two teams met in Umbria and Perugia won an ill-fated match by two goals to one. The night before the game a group of Perugia fans roughened up some Toro players in a hotel and the match itself, thanks in part to regular Italian football hardman Marco Materazzi, was a black and blue experience. Consequently, the two teams finished the regular season level on points and under the rules of that year, were forced to play-off a one-off match to decide the fourth team promoted to the top-flight.

The tie was played under intense heat in Reggio Emilia, Perugia fans were hosed with cold water, Toro fans left to melt. As the teams entered the pitch the Perugini displayed the untactful 'A pair of Superga's' banner, a poisonous reference to the Torino air disaster (Superga also being a popular brand of Italian shoes).

The game was typically volatile and after four minutes Toro were reduced to ten-men after the perm haired Fabio Tricarico was dismissed for an apparent elbow by sunburnt referee Graziano Cesari. Such conditions usually suit Toro, adversity and agony, and typically the team battled back, recovering from a goal down to draw 1-1. The match went to penalties. Nine were converted perfectly. One hit the post, that belonging to former England international Tony Dorigo, Torino's left-back. Perugia proceeded to celebrate promotion in their truly tactful style.

Seven years on and Perugia had spent most of the subsequent years in Serie A, Toro continued to yo-yo between the two divisions, too good for one, too bad for the other. Lady luck, however, seemed to be on Torino's side this time around. Both teams had finished the season on 74 points in joint third-place and narrowly behind the two automatically promoted teams - Genoa and Empoli. However, Torino had the advantage in the play-offs having taken four points out of six against Perugia in the league and thus guaranteeing home advantage in the second-leg and the right to gain promotion should the tie be drawn after extra time in the return match.

The days leading up to the first-leg harboured too many memories of 1998 - and the presence of ex-Gobbi[3] Fabrizio Ravanelli and Davide

---

[3] A Gobbo is used to describe a supporter or player of the 'other team', translating literally as hunchback. The phrase is derived from the Bianconeri's

Baiocco in the Perugia squad, threats of violence between the two sets of fans (which mercifully didn't materialise) and ill-timed comments of former Perugia Coach Illario Castagner - further intensified the build-up to the big-match.

The first-leg was played on a Thursday evening. 6,000 Toro fans made the long trip down to Umbria, unfortunately I was confined to watching the game inside a pub in the centre of Turin, paying six euros to watch the match in a room below the main bar, on the floor reserved for pool tables. The room tucked away in a hidden corner looks rather like a 1930s cinema where a big screen shows Torino matches. The room is poorly lit and when entering you have no sense of where the seats are, how many people are present or if the audio will actually work. And that's six euros without a beer. Supporters of the 'other team' can usually watch the games in the bar upstairs, paying for what they consume not for the pleasure of watching their championship winning team. There's nothing like being a second-class citizen. The room was filled with the usual range of pessimistic old men and thirtysomethings who pick a player each to abuse - usually the best players on the pitch.

The game was played under a heavy June downpour and some sections of the open stadium were vacant. Toro, guided by Renato Zaccarelli, a hero of the 1976 Scudetto winning team, presented a prudent formation with a lone attacker - the Count Massimo Marazzina - and supported by the team's occasionally talented and often podgy Brazilian playmaker Andrè Pinga.

Zac went old-school selecting a side which presented itself with a 5-4-1 formation and covering up the suspensions to regulars like Gianluca Comotto and captain Diego De Ascentis. Comotto had sensibly ruled himself out of the final by gobbing on an opponent in the semi-final with the game already won.

Zac's tactics paid off and Toro produced a performance of rare conviction away from home. One gallop down the right and reserve right-back Francesco Carbone supplied an inch-perfect cross which delivered itself to the foot of the left-wing-back Federico Balzaretti, the fan's idol and Torino youth product, who jabbed the ball under goalkeeper Lorenzo

---

formation when playing with a pink shirt in the early 20th century their players seemed like hunchbacks when in motion.

Squizzi from 10 yards. 0-1. Perugia pressed and right on the stroke of half-time predictably equalised. An offside trap not of Arsenal nor Full Monty standards was easily breached and rat-faced Federico Massara equalised. 1-1.

This is usually where Toro capitulate, surrendering the game, spurning chances and conceding a late winner. Zac, however, installed confidence and conviction in his side and the team came out for the second-half looking for the killer goal. Pinga found that extra yard of pace which he'd frustratingly reserved all season, Romanian Paul Codrea discovered the art of tackling and Alessandro Conticchio retention of possession.

After one of Pinga's inspired counter-attacks, Toro earned a corner. The ball rebounded back to the Brazilian whose cross met the head of the Count who despite seeing his first effort saved smashed home the rebound and the team charged under the large away support to celebrate. 1-2. Perugia were gone. Long, aimless balls were easily swept and the introduction of Ravanelli as a second-half substitute, only confused matters. Unbelievably, Toro had delivered and the pre-San Giovanni[4] celebrations in the city that night had an extra satisfaction.

Between the two games were four, very long days. The team was so convincing in Perugia to be true. The break would enable Perugia to regroup and discover that 'nothing to lose' mentality. Instead for Toro, and because of their history, only doubts would creep in. What if we went a goal-down early on? How do we approach the game? Will Zac play with two forwards? Will the players relax? Will they be too tense?

I took off to the Lago di Garda between the two games, unable to cope with the tension, stress and expectancy created in the city for the match. The result, naturally, would have a major influence on the future of the club given the financial benefits of playing in Serie A. Toro legend Aldo Agroppi perfectly summed up the days between the two matches when admitting: 'Even taking my dog for a walk or playing tennis can't eleviate the stress. The game is on my mind all the time.'

For the first time in ten years, Torino sold out a game. The Stadio Delle Alpi which is grey, unpopular, isolated from the city and poorly designed

---

[4] San Giovanni, is the patron saint of Torino and the 24th June is a city holiday.

was for once a spectrum of beauty for an evening. The 'other team', the 'most popular team in Italy™', who had just won the Scudetto and played Champions' League matches that same year against Real Madrid and Liverpool were unable to command such a public.

The Curva Maratona, the second tier of the Curva Nord and home to the oldest ultrà group in Italy (the Fedelissimi), sold-out immediately first followed by the third tier of the same stand and the Curva Sud (usual home of the 'other team'). The tribunes rapidly sold-out and parts of the ground which are seldomly used that they are never even open. Some seats probably still have the Italia '90 stickers attached[5].

Even arriving two hours before the game was not enough to guarantee a seat in the curva. Both the second and third tier were crammed with people occupying the isles. There was not a space to be had. The construction of the stadium is to blame as from at least 50% of the first tier you are below pitch level. Consequently, visibility is terrible and fans fight for space on the top two tiers. There is no control over where people sit even at the risk of tragedy, with the overcrowding of some areas. In Italy there is no place like the curva. Whilst 80% of the stadium has the right to remain placid, the curva is an open-air disco that carries a serious public health warning.

An hour before kick-off, the stadium was already shaking and almost everyone was dressed in burgundy. Some fans had obviously not been to the stadium before, moaning about not being able to sit in the exact seat number displayed on their ticket, others about the scarce lack of refreshments and toilets.

The Stadio Delle Alpi, a UFO of a stadium, is vast. If you happen to park or get off a bus at the wrong side of the stadium, it can take you up to 15 minutes to get around the other side and its a stadium without a reference point or a distinguishing feature. The perimeter fence surrounding the stadium is ridiculously far away from the ground, almost like the bailey of a castle, and indeed once past the turnstiles there is a steady descent up from the moat to the second and third tiers of the stadium. It desperately lacks facilities. There are two refreshment bars in

---

[5] The Stadio Delle Alpi was officially opening in 1990 and constructed for the FIFA World Cup that same year. It has since been home to Torino and the team who play in black & white striped shirts. Neither club particularly like it.

the Curva Nord, both of which stopped selling alcohol in time for the 2004-05 season, the only ground in Italy to do so, and somewhat surprising since Torino were sponsored at the time by the Bavaria Holland Beer company!

The range of refreshments are laughable, and Italian football lacks the Bovril & pie culture of its English counterpart. There is coffee burnt so intensely it resembles charcoaled gravy, a few dodgy rolls and a choice of a KitKat or a Mars. There is no chance of getting what you want (a) if you have respect for the queuing system and (b) have anything larger than a five euro note. And like anywhere in Italy, it's one queue for the till and another for the goods. Hardly conducive to a fifteen minute half-time break.

There is still no concept of merchandising or bleeding fans dry for their money. There are no programmes, a mere giveaway newspaper called *StudioSport*, the only shirts, scarves, badges, stickers available are those of the ultrà groups or fake specials outside the ground where PINGA '10' mingles with dyslexic specialities like GERARD '4', SCHEVCHENKO '7' and LEMPARD '8'. Admittedly, there are three Torino stores in the centre of town, but you have to be looking for them to find them and ominously the 'other team' are one of few Italian clubs to have embraced the concept of merchandising, opening a store at the Caselle Airport and in via Garibaldi, the latter a preferred spot for vandalism by some Torino ultras, and the former a cunning way of spreading the 'other team's' global power.

The toilets in the Delle Alpi are also something unbelievable. Another reason for going to the game at least an hour before kick-off is that you will still probably be able to enter the toilets without losing your feet under a sea of piss and flem. Toilet paper and a sink basin remain an occasional, luxurious extra.

Tonight, you don't want to go to the toilet or more profusely, you can't. Move a muscle and someone has budged into your place. The whole evening is a battle to stop some guy, who has not been to the stadium all season, telling you to vacate your place because he has a ticket with your seat number printed on it or avoid too much physical contact with the person sitting next to you who invariably is smoking something either illegal or horrendous, or horrendously illegal and blowing it in your direction, farting, burping, sweating and wanting to engage in inane conversation every time you catch his eye, or even when you don't.

The players come out an hour before kick-off and understandably are a little unsure of how to react. This is not Triestina in December nor Pescara in March. Usually only the Maratona is full, with little patches of the stadium showing some life. Tonight, an hour before the kick-off the place is pumping. There are television cameras everywhere, the giant Torino mascot, the Toro (Bull) sits proudly and aggressively under the Maratona after years in retirement, and at least one of the scoreboards is actually working. The evening is humid, dry and energy sapping.

'Keeper Stefano Sorrentino is the first out to receive a unanimous ovation 'Soren-teen-o Olè Olè', Soren-teen-o Olè Olè . The rest emerge to limber up near the corner flag. The atmosphere is unsurprisingly tense. A 2-1 lead for most teams would be an advantage, for Toro no. There is almost a sensation that it would be better to be facing a 2-1 deficit. As per form, only the eleven first-teamers train, the substitutes warm-up to one side. It's clear Zac has gone negative, maintain what we've got, let them take the game to us. Suicide tactics.

Carbone is out there. Conticchio is out there. Marazzina is the only forward. It's a team packed with midfielders and built to contain. Perugia players take a walk on the pitch, first in their suits and a little later in sync with the arrival of the 2-3,000 or so supporters, to warm-up. It's the longest build-up to a game I've experienced, the tension is palpable, you feel yourself shake, your heart burn and try in vain to tell yourself that it's only a game and a defeat won't ruin the rest of your life.

Eventually the teams come out to a sea of granata and white flags and a giant banner folded in the tribune opposite the tunnel. Under the stadium lights, the claret shirts and flags look even more intense, romantic and passionate. Perugia, in contrast, in their non-descript white shirts and red shorts fade into the background.

Before the first leg, Perugia had won nine games in a row and had the best away record in Serie B. This was not an easy obstacle. Toro started nervously, passes which players could usually make blindfolded went astray, there were a series of foul-throws and lack of coordination about both teams. The Count went close to scoring early before his shot rickashade away for a corner.

However, Perugia began to grow in confidence and in possession. And this supremacy soon reaped its reward. During one of a series of corners, the ball broke to the edge of the box and after a flap by Sorrentino, the Lion from Congo and tamed in Belgium, Gabi Mudingayi, pulled out of a tackle for the first time all season, allowing Mascara to pinch the ball and slot into the unmarked post from 12 yards. 0-1. 2-2 on aggregate. Advantage Toro, but by a whisker.

Torino struggled desperately in the first-half to re-establish themselves in the game. Mudingayi, Conticchio and De Ascentis kicked, ran and conceded possession in equal measure. Neither Carbone nor Balzaretti dared venture forward. Maurizio Peccarisi played dangerous with possession in his own penalty area, Pinga never saw the ball and only Marazzina looked particularly dangerous. Indeed, I Grifoni almost came close to doubling their lead when Stendardo's header was palmed over the bar. Toro eventually managed to string three passes together in the five minutes before the interval.

The half-time whistle was a welcome rest bite as much for the fans as the team who had spent the first-half in good voice but in need of some evidence from the team that this wouldn't be the latest chapter of failure. Zac resisted the temptation of introducing a second forward and Toro began the second-half with the same XI who finished the first period. The second period was even worse than the first. Perugia held most of the possession without threatening but Toro struggled to get out of their own-half nor offer the fans any relief. As long as the game developed, we feared for the worse.

I Grifoni won corner after corner and their fans began to make their voices heard. The Toro resistance was pure resistance, the back-five holding a tight line and resisted in clearing Perugia's predictable attempts to puncture it. Ravanelli came on but again was to make no impact apart from receiving the kind of reception usually reserved for convicted paedophiles.

However, there was one moment when the dream seemed over. Antonio Floro Flores, a mouthful of a name, drove through the Torino defence, beat two men and found himself on the edge of the six-yard box. Instead of feeding an unmarked colleague he made one turn too many allowing Luca Mezzano to make the most almighty of challenges. A major turning point. The final ten minutes of normal time took an age. Ferdinand Coly pounded and muscled his way past the brilliant but puny Balzaretti down the right-flank but thankfully delivered no end product. Eventually, the full-time whistle blew and some fans celebrated Serie A, unaware that the positional rule, which favoured Toro, was only applied after 120 minutes.

Zac introduced veteran Pippo Maniero for Pinga in extra-time and Maniero would batter and bruise the Perugia defence for 30 minutes, retaining possession and taking the sting out of the game. The usually sleepy Curva Sud even began encouraging the rest of the stadium with cries of 'Toro, Toro, Toro', which harked back to epic matches of the 1970s. Perugia were gone, their final efforts tired and immune and unlike the final ten minutes of normal time, extra time carried a kind of strange safety-blanket, a feeling that it was too late. Perugia wouldn't score and didn't.

In the final minute of the game, Mudingayi was sent-off for a second bookable offence. Good. Another 15 seconds gone. Another 15 seconds later, we were in Serie A. The relief was replaced with ecstasy, Perugia were reminded who won, who were in Serie A and how long their journey home was. Revenge.

The players charged under the curva, initially in unison and then in groups to thank the fans individually. Pinga and reserve 'keeper / ultrà Alberto Fontana danced on the Bull, De Ascentis displayed his tattooed six-pack, a group of fans wrestled with some Perugia players and Zac was carried under the curva.

The party continued long into the early hours in the centre of town. Piazza Castello, which a month earlier had witnessed the 'other team' display the league championship ala inglese on an open top bus, became an open-air dance floor for the evening. Teenagers stripped to their pants, danced for joy, others displayed a charming banner reading: 'You've got The Gaucci, we've got Eva Henger.'[6] The older school supporters proudly scanned copies of *La Stampa*, hot off the press, others drove around like maniacs with their hand firmly on the horn. It

---

[6] Luciano Gaucci is the President of Perugia, a vulcano of a man, who provokes little affection from supporters of rival teams. Eva Henger, an ex-Hungarian playgirl, now an Italian TV star and Torino fan.

was our chance to keep the Gobbi awake and the Granata party lasted well into the early hours of the morning.

Chapter 2 - Superga, Meroni, Ferrini

Key dates in the story of Torino Calcio:

1906 Club formed in Bar Norman, Piazza Solferino.

1927 'First' Scudetto revoked for alleged 'match-fixing' - a game won against the 'other team'!

1928 Toro are Champions of Italy for the first time.

1936 Torino win their first Coppa Italia.

1939 Feruccio Novo takes over the club and lays the foundations for Il Grande Torino.

1943 Il Grande Torino win the Coppa Italia. In the same year they claim a second league title. Serie A is then suspended until 1945-46.

1946-49 Il Grande Torino win another three championships in a row.

1949 Superga Air Disaster. No survivors. Italy's greatest ever club side perishes. Shortly after which Torino are awarded their fifth straight Italian title, fielding the youth team in their remaining four games.

1956 Torino Calcio become Torino Talmone for two years.

1959 Torino are relegated to Serie B for the first time, returning a year later.

1961 Denis Law and Joe Baker crash into a tree after a drunken night out in Turin and although survive, their Torino careers don't.

1963 Orfeo Pianelli begins his 20-year stint as club President.

1967 Gigi Meroni dies in a road accident at the age of 24. A week later Torino win the derby 4-0 in his memory.

1968 Torino claim their third domestic cup title, their first major success after Superga.

1971 Coppa Italia No 4 is claimed after a penalty shoot-out win over Milan.

1976 Torino win their 7th (8th) and last title thanks to the exploits of Pulici, Claudio Sala, Graziani et al. The club's longest serving player, Giorgio Ferrini dies of a brain haemorrhage at the age of 37.

1983 Torino come from 2-0 down to score three goals in three minutes and defeat the black-and-white striped team in the derby. Sergio Rossi replaces Pianelli as club President.

1989 I Granata are relegated to Serie B for only the second time. Gianmarco Borsano takes over as President of the club.

1990 Toro leave the Stadio Comunale for the newly designed Stadio Delle Alpi.

1992 Toro lose the UEFA Cup Final to Ajax. Gigi Lentini joins Milan for a world record £13 million.

1993 Torino beat Roma in the Coppa Italia final, the club's last major honour.

1995 In a horrific year which ends in relegation to Serie B. I Granata also become the first Serie A team to play in peach.

2002 Torino come from 3-0 down in the derby to draw 3-3, claiming Serie A survival.

2003 The club are again relegated to Serie B, finishing bottom of Serie A after a disastrous campaign.

2005 Torino Calcio are pronounced clinically dead. On 1 September, Urbano Cairo becomes President of the new Torino Football Club.

No club in Italy, perhaps not the world, carries a history as tragic, proud and resilient as that of Torino Calcio. A football club without middle measures, never mundane or an object of indifference. A phrase often heard on Italian television, particularly RAI, is: 'We all want Torino to do well and see them return to where they should be. No team represents more poignantly the history of Italian football.'

Torino's history is powerful, emotive and beautiful. The club is unrivalled for drama, tragedy, suspense and sufferance. The beautiful moments have been made more beautiful by the long years of suffering in between, indeed some of the sufferance has almost become beautiful.

Here in fact lies the crux of the problem, the heavyweight of history has not only paralysed Torino from moving forward but is also a convenient way of pigeon-holeing Toro as a chapter in the past, a collectable and admired piece of football nostalgia, a romantic reminder of yesteryear, an unwelcome elderly relative in the world of TV contracts, million dollar contracts and the Champions' League.

As black and white Director General Luciano Moggi recently claimed to the wrath of Toro fans: "Turin is too big for two teams yet Torino's history is too powerful and beautiful for the club to disappear." Moggi and his Bianconeri counterpart, the second member of the 'other team's' triad, Antonio Giraudo, a Torino supporter, have long seen Toro's presence as a factor in their club's failure to fill a stadium and maximise their marketing potential. Unsurprisingly, Torino's fans also agree that Turin is too small for two teams.

Torino fans are quite rightly a pessimistic bunch but also a passionate group as well. The blood-coloured shirts represent a passion, intensity and liveliness unrivalled, the Curva Maratona one of Italy's most passionate and colourful, home to the oldest ultrà group - the Fedelissimi dating back to 1952 - and many of Italy's historic ultrà groups.

The people of Turin support Torino, and it's regularly said that the Torinese are cold, impassionate and practical. Almost paradoxically, Torino fans are the opposite of supporters from the north and almost have the splendour, noise and colour of a club from the south. Although, a real 'Torinese' is a Torino fan, supporter groups of the club can be found all over Italy and the world, and it's a common assumption to limit Torino's web to Turin, as the summer of 2005 proved.

Torino Calcio were formed in 1906 - on the 3rd December to be precise - ten years after their bitter rivals in a pub called the Birriera Voigt in via Pietro Micca, now called Bar Norman, by a group of dissidents from the 'other team' in the city. However, whilst rivals ***ventus were formed in the 1890s, so too effectively were Torino, under the guise Club Torinese, a team though which ran into serious financial difficulties.

The fruits of this club were to inspire the creation of Torino Calcio. Twenty-three business partners, mainly Swiss, founded the new club electing Hans Schoenbrod as President. Even 100 years earlier, Piemontese businessman were not amongst the first in the queue to buy the club. The first victory arrived in Torino's first match, a 3-1 derby win over Pro Vercelli. The goalscorers were Rodgers, Michel and an own goal. Arthur Rodgers, Torino's first ever marksman was an Englishman, known for his bravery and in a infamous match a few years later he played with a broken arm before being sent-off.

The club played its home matches at the Umberto I velodrome, now a hospital, and had a new President in 1907, the imaginatively named Alfred Dick, a Swiss manufacturer who had been responsible for the foundation of **ve. He'd fallen out with his former club and was one of the catalysts behind the foundation of Torino Calcio. Dick, though, would not last long (he had craved the position as President to get one over on his former associates) and was soon replaced by Giovanni Secondi, the first Italian patron of the club. In 1912 Torino even had a full-time coach in the shape of Vittorio Pozzo, who became a legendary figure in the 1930s, guiding Italy to two World Cups in 1934 and 1938. Pozzo enjoyed a lengthy and successful spell, remaining at the helm until 1922.

By 1914, Toro were playing at a new venue in the Piazza d'Armi and became one of the first European clubs to embark on a triumphant South American tour, visiting Brazil (where they won every game) and Argentina, something which even for the present club would be unthinkable.

In 1914-15, the Granata perhaps suffered the first piece of misfortune characteristic of their history. Trailing league leaders Genoa by two points with two games to go, Toro prepared for a head-to-head against the Rossoblu which could have been crucial in the side's march for a first championship. However, Italy's entrance into the Great War saw the championship cancelled and Genoa declared arbitrary champions.

Putting the misfortune into context, Torino had hammered Genoa 4-0 in the fixture earlier that season. The Italian championship was indeed halted for a number of years, and many Torino players were conscripted to a war from which they never returned.

In the early 1920s, Toro began to gain strength as a club and featured in the final phases of the championships although Pozzo was forced to leave the club in 1922 due to family problems and was replaced as coach by the Austrian Karl Sturmer. Conte Enrico Marone Cinzano, he of the pretentious drink, became President in 1924 and financed some interesting signings like Julio Libonatti and Adolfo Baloncieri, united with a number of talented local players.

Under Cinzano, things were seldom dull especially due to his wealth, noble background and international standing. He funded the construction of the club's first real stadium with the building of the Stadio Filadelfia, a venue inaugurated in 1926. The new stadium was located in the south of the city, close to the FIAT headquarters.

A year later, the club would be embroiled in its first major scandal. After a sensational season, Torino were proclaimed champions of Italy, only to have the title revoked, a decision still contested today. Unsurprisingly, the problem revolved around a disputed derby game. A Bianconeri player, the fullback Gigi Allemandi, was alleged by journalists to have been offered money to lose the match by a Torino official, a match Toro won 2-1.

The allegations of match fixing stood despite some controversial and loose evidence. Allemandi was considered man-of-the-match and alleged to have changed his mind before the game. A Torino director, Dr Nani, later confessed to the allegations although the title was never awarded to another club and was indeed revoked four months after Torino won the title and whilst the following season was underway! Torino have spent years trying through legal channels to reclaim that title. Cinzano never digested the decision, although he cemented his reputation as first great President of the club.

Within a year, Toro were Italy's premiere club. The side were coached by Tony Cargnelli, who although had Austrian ancestors, broke Toro's spell of foreign coaches, predominantly Austrians, Swiss and Germans. Patience proved a virtue and after twice coming close Torino were champions - taking the title at a canter, inspired by the anger of having the title stripped a year earlier and by a prolific forward line of Libonatti, Baloncieri and Gino Rossetti who scored 89 goals between them. Also significant, was the return from injury of Antonio Janni, who would become a stalwart of the club. A year later Toro would narrowly miss out on another title, losing a play-off against Bologna.

The 1930s would witness the domination of Italian football of the team from the other side of the city, greater professionalism and a league format similar to the current Serie A, inaugurated in 1929-30. Torino, themselves, would go through a succession of Presidents, with a change at the helm almost every two years. It was also the era of Pozzo's strong Italian national team thanks to its South American 'Oriundi' connection and the Granata also fielded a number of South Americans.

The club suffered a scare in 1935 when having to beat Livorno on the final day of the season to avoid relegation to Serie B. Torino recovered from that near shock to feature in the upper echelons of the game, thanks to an emerging youth policy - these players were known as the Balon Boys - even taking their first of five Italian Cups in 1936, with an emphatic win over Alessandria. The Stadio Filadelfia had a change of name in this period, becoming the Stadio Mussolini. Two seasons later Torino finished a credible third place in the league. In 1937, again at the orders of Mussolini, Torino Football Club became Torino Associazione Calcio, due to Il Duce's desire to eradicate foreign sounding names.

The beginning of a glorious era for the club commenced in 1939 with the arrival of Ferruccio Novo as President. Novo would construct the greatest Italian club side of all time, piecing together a number of intelligent and expensive signings. Novo, Turin born and an ambitious and modern figure had major plans for Torino wanting to create a superteam. Novo wanted to build Torino on the English model of a club, with a staff of collaborators with specific roles and a greater dedication to training and tactics. Hence throughout his reign of President, the introduction of athletic coaches, technical gurus, a tactics expert and a regular switching of staff despite the success of the team. He also welcomed foreign coaches who could pass on modern methods to the players. He believed in keeping a close group of people together and basing his relationships on trust.

His first choice as coach was Mario Sperone with the Hungarian Egri Ernest Egri Erbstein as technical director. The talented Hungarian gained some impressive early results before leaving Italy to protect his family due to the threats made during the Second World War against Jews. He would return to great success years later and was replaced in the short-term by compatriot Ferenc Molnar.

Novo's first signing was Franco Ossola from Varese, a player recommended by former player Janni, then coach of Varese. The forward enjoyed a promising first season with the club, scoring 15 times. Ossola was joined by the midfielder Romeo Menti from Fiorentina, Giuseppe Grezar from Triestina who together with Guglielmo 'The Baron' Gabetto from the 'other team' formed the early nucleus of the side. After finishing seventh in 1940-41, Torino earned a credible second place finish in 1941-42 just behind champions Roma. The club went through a succession of coaches, after Molnar arrived Andrea Mattea before Andrea Kutik, another man of Hungarian origin was hired. The loss, albeit temporary, of Erbstein was palpable.

Novo continued to invest heavily, piecing together his two major signings in the summer of 1942 with the acquisitions of Valentino Mazzola and Ezio Loik from Venezia, two of the most highly rated young players in Italy. He was also, thanks to his excellent collaborators, able to promote his own ethos for the club, creating a friendly atmosphere far from the austere President-player relationships of the 1930s, where respect counted both on and off the pitch.

During the start of the 1942-43 season, Janni, already a club legend, having played 324 times for Toro, replaced Andrea Kutik as Coach and helped steer the team to the title following a win against Bari on Easter weekend in 1943. In Mazzola and Loik's first year together in Turin and thanks to a fantastic second-half of the campaign, Torino edged out Livorno for the title.

A month later, the side claimed the only domestic double in the club's history, with Mazzola on the scoresheet in a Cup Final victory over his former club, Venezia. The Coppa Italia then ceased to exist until 1958, a pity considering the number of trophies that the club could have won.

Due to the war, the 1943-1944 season was annulled although an unofficial championship was created with Torino taking the name Torino-

Fiat, due to the motor company's decision to help keep the Torino team together by offering jobs to the players during the war. The team even borrowed Italian football legend Silvio Piola for the tournament.

Despite the presence of Piola, Gabetto and Mazzola, Torino were defeated in the final by a team of La Spezia firemen in the final. This unofficial championship and major embarrassment has thankfully become only a footnote in the history of Il Grande Torino. The excuse for the shock defeat was that a number of players were tired from playing a game for the national team in Trieste. Even sixty years later some things have not changed.

The real Torino team was strong yet still in its moulding phase and resumed full activity after the war. In the 1945-46 campaign, for which they entire back-line was replaced, they scored 104 goals in 38 league games, this time coached by Luigi Ferrero and Erbstein who had moved back to the city following the end of the global conflict. The most monumental result of the season was a 7-0 victory at Roma, when Toro led 6-0 after 19 minutes!

With strong new additions like 'keeper Valerio Bacigalupo, the Ballarin brothers (Dino followed Aldo in 1948), Virgilio Maroso and Mario Rigamonti the team was reinforced in all areas. This marked the beginnings of the superteam which in 1946-47 scored 104 goals, conceding just 35. A classic example of the side's strength was evident in a home match against Bologna. The opposition arrived at the Filadelfia having taken 13 out of the 14 points available since the start of the season. They left Turin with their tales firmly beneath their legs, suffering a 4-0 defeat.

The club smashed all scoring records and gave the sensation that whatever the situation, they were capable of winning a match. A team with sublime technique and awesome athleticism, all the names of this side are etched on the minds of all Italian football connoisseurs.

Indeed in May 1947, they were etched on the mind of Italy boss Pozzo who selected 10 Torino players - a record - for an international match against Hungary. Only goalkeeper Valerio Bacagliupo was left out, although he would gain international recognition soon after. Torino, sorry, Italy won 3-2 with a brace from Gabetto and a goal by Loik.

The strong team of 1946-47 was replaced by even more incredible line-up during the 1947-48 season, with Sperone as coach and Roberto Copernico as technical director, a campaign which had saw Mazzola and Gabetto grab 48 goals between them. The side claimed 65 points in 40 games, dropping just 15 of the points on offer, scored 125 goals, finished 16 points ahead of second placed Milan, **ve and Triestina, recorded a 10-0 home win over Alessandria, scored at least five goals or more on twelve occasions and gained a total of 29 wins in 40 games.

The beginning of that year had seen some significant changes at the top with Mario Sperone replacing Ferrero as the technical director, who coupled with Erbstein's tactical genius formed a forward thinking, athletic and tactically interchangeable side. The club had a number of interchangeable collaborators yet this never spoiled the mechanics of the club.

Torino prepared for the following season with the introduction of three promising young players in Operto, Grava and the Hungarian midfielder Schubert. Perhaps more significant was the arrival of the English athletic coach Leslie Lievesley, who worked side by side with Erbstein and the side again dominated the championship thanks to its unstoppable attack, formidable strength and ability to change gears at will. Captain Mazzola became the greatest player of his age, closely followed by Gabetto, Loik and Ossola.

Il Grande Torino won five consecutive Italian titles, only war was able to interrupt an even greater sequence. The side never lost a home match at the mythical Stadio Filadelfia, where when the team needed a lift, the club's legendary trumpeter, Bormida, would respond from the stands and inspire Mazzola et all to another victory. A famous example was a game against Lazio in May 1948, with Toro 3-0 down after twenty minutes, running out 4-3 winners with a brace from Castigliano and goals from Gabetto and Mazzola. That same summer, Il Grande Torino visited Brazil, such was their worldwide standing and international reputation.

Mazzola was the obvious symbol of the team, his famous gesture of rolling his sleeves up to mark the 'quarta d'ora granata - 'the famous 15 minutes' when the team needed the extra push. A man who caused a scandal with the discovery that he had two families and two children to different women, was an elegant and decisive captain, who led by example. His aura was such that when it seemed he would have to join

Inter to finance his two families, his team-mates renounced their win bonus to help him stay in Turin. By 1949, the shape of Il Grande Torino had formed and the team reads like a chorus: Bacigalupo, Ballarin, Maroso, Martelli, Rigamonti, Castigliano, Menti, Loik, Gabetto, Mazzola, Ossola.

It was side too strong to be beaten, a side which has always remained imperious, young and formidable due to its tragic end. On the 4th May 1949, Torino were returning from an international friendly against Benfica in Lisbon, a match organised by the captains of the two sides who met during an Italy versus Portugal international match. The Benfica skipper Jose Ferreira was about to retire and wanted to bow out against Mazzola's Torino.

On the return journey from Portugal, dense fog surrounded the hills of Turin, and the plane unable to land at the city's airport began to make a diversion for Milan. It was a diversion it was never able to make. Pilot Pierluigi Meroni lost visibility and the plane crashed into the hill near the side of the Basilica di Superga, the imperious monument which sits on the hill overlooking Turin, built as a defence against the French army 200 years earlier. Between 17:01 and 17:04, Il Grande Torino perished.

There were no survivors. All players, journalists, coaching staff and club employers were killed. A distraught Pozzo, national team boss and former Torino coach, was left to identify the bodies. Only those who remained in Turin, including reserve-team player Sandro Toma, survived although they were left to mourn. Many left young or unborn children. Turin mourned and the funeral was not only a day of local but national mourning. Weeks after the Superga tragedy, the club claimed its fifth straight Italian title as the youth team played out the remaining fixtures against opposition youth sides, the first just 11 days after the tragedy.

Il Grande Torino had given strength, vigour and pride to a nation destroyed and without identity after the Second World War. It was another bitter blow for a country already decimated and for Torino a tragedy which would define and shape the club's future existence. Il Grande Torino represented everything sport should - fairness, excellence, dedication and respect.

Il Grande Torino

Valerio Bacigalupo. Born 12/1/1924. Age 25

Il Grande Torino's goalkeeper remains one of the most underrated players of that side, perhaps due to his introverted character. Signed from Genoa in 1945, only injury in the 1946-47 season interrupted his sequence between the posts. Making 137 appearances for the club, he conceded just 115 goals and made five national team appearances.

Aldo Ballarin. Born 10/1/22. Age 27

More celebrated than his younger brother Dino, the senior Ballarin featured 148 times for Torino. A classic full-back he was renowned for his tough-tackling and a bullish spirit. A national team regular under Pozzo, he made his Torino debut in a derby in 1945.

Dino Ballairn. Born 23/9/24. Age 25

Like his older brother, Ballarin hailed from the town of Chioggia. However, he was a 'keeper and signed as cover for Bacigalupo and second-choice Gandolfi. He never played a first-team match.

Virgilio Maroso. Born 26/6/25. Age 23

One of the younger members of the squad, having been noticed playing in his native Veneto by the club's talent scouts. Maroso, joined Toro's youth team, before graduating to the first team in 1945, making 103 appearances for the club.

Mario Rigamonti. Born 17/12/22 Age 26

A rebellious character, famed for riding motorbikes, who despite his indiscretions never let the side down, and became the central figure of the defence. Rigamonti also made his debut in a derby game and became a regular in the national team. Born in Brescia, he was signed from his home-town club, where the team's stadium now bears his name.

Ezio Loik. Born 26/1/19 Age 30

Loik was born just eight months after Mazzola and like the Il Grande Torino captain, he would make his mark at Venezia following a spell with Milan. A similar player to Kevin Keegan, a hard worker who had made the most out of his talents. He was not only one of the founder members of Il Grande Torino, but one of the most consistent. Loik could always be relied on for goals, as his 62 strikes in 160 games prove.

Giuseppe Grezar Born 25/11/18 Age 30

One of the more experienced members of the side, and another consistent performer who was more noticeable on the pitch than off it. The classic team player, who was signed from Triestina, Grezar held the midfield together notching 19 goals in 154 matches.

Eusebio Castigliano Born 9/2/21 Age 28

Castigliano joined Toro after the Second World War from Spezia. More of a flair player than Grezar, the two complemented each other, Castigliano being a more skilful if not less aggressive performer, who particularly enjoyed the derby matches where his ruthless streak was evident. Castigliano was a regular goalscorer, scoring 35 times in 116 games.

Danilo Martelli. Born 27/5/23 Age 25

Martelli joined Torino in 1946 was he was at university training to be a doctor. Although never the first name on the team sheet, his versatility earning him 12th man status. The club overturned offers to sell him and the modest Martelli enjoyed his role as a reserve at a great club and consequently never played for the national team. In his three years at Torino, he scored 10 times in 72 matches.

Franco Ossola Born 23/8/21 Age 27

Ossola, arriving from his native Varese, was the first major signing under Novo. A winger of pace, and an eye for goal as his 86 goals for the club testify, Ossola was an indispensable member of the side, noted for his fair-play and importance in the dressing room.

Romeo Menti Born 5/9/19 Age 29

A player of extreme pace and energy, Menti played on the opposite flank to Ossola and was one of the players most feared by the opposition. Menti was the team's dead-ball specialist and designated penalty taker, and another member of the side renowned for his introverted character and calm temperament. Menti scored 53 times in 131 appearances.

Guglielmo Gabetto, Born 24/2/16. Age 33.

No player scored more goals for Il Grande Torino than the veteran of the team. Gabetto began his career with the city's other team, scoring almost 100 goals for the Bianconeri. In the summer of 1941, he was put up for sale and Novo promptly made one of his most astute signings. Gabetto went onto score over 120 goals for Torino, most of them exquisite. The Baron was once stopped after a friendly in Switzerland for filling his suitcases with contraband cigarettes.

Valentino Mazzola 26/1/19 Age 30

Although the Grande Torino side was formidable due to the strength of the squad and revolutionary tactics, Mazzola became the symbol of the side. Mazzola joined Torino with Loik in the summer of 1942, Novo beating off strong competition from ***entus. Mazzola proved an inspirational leader, commanding respect off the pitch and acting as a conductor on it. Mazzola played in a classic role just behind the forwards and his class saw him score 97 times in 170 appearances. His greatest asset was his leadership and ability to get the best out of his team-mates when things were down.

Pietro Operto Born 20/12/26 Age 22

Essentially signed as a reserve to Maroso in the summer of 1948 from Casale before making 11 appearances for the club. A local-born player who had a bright future ahead of him.

Rubens Fadini Born 1/6/27 Age 21

Signed as a potential heir to Castigliano, Fadini like Operto was signed in the summer of 1948 as one of the players for whom a great future was built. Sadly, he was to make only ten appearances.

Julius Schubert Born 12/12/22 Age 26

A Hungarian winger requested specifically by Erbstein, Schubert had few opportunities to shine, featuring just five times as understudy to Mazzola.

Ruggero Grava Born 26/4/22 Age 27

A squad player signed from the French team Roubaix, Grava featured just once in the Granata shirt.

Emile Bongiorni. Born 19/3/21 Age 28

Another one of the clutch of players signed in the summer of 1948, whose 'bedding in' season at the club would prove his last. The French attacker scored twice in eight appearances.

Also perished: Arnaldo Agnisetta, Ippolito Civalleri, Egri Erbstein, Leslie Lievesley, Ottavio Cortina (masseur), Renato Casalbore (Tuttosport, journalist), Luigi Cavallero (La Stampa, journalist), Renato Tosatti (Gazzetta del Popolo, journalist); Andrea Boniauti (organiser), Pierluigi Meroni (flight captain), Antonio Pangrazi, Celestino D'Inca, Cesare Biancardi.

Every May 4th, fans make the pilgrimage to Superga to pay tribute to the team at the memorial outside the Basilica. It has become a place of deep spiritual significance for Torino supporters, rather like the Filadelfia. After the 1976 Scudetto triumph, over 200,000 people are said to have made the trip to pay their tributes. Superga's 50-year anniversary was commemorated in 1999 with a match between the present Torino side and heroes of the past at the Stadio Delle Alpi, in weather conditions eerily similar to those of 1949.

Had the Superga tragedy not occurred, nobody can imagine where Torino would be today. The team was at the peak of its powers and had enough to win another two or three titles at a canter, thus guaranteeing the gold star awarded for teams who have won more then ten titles. European football began in the mid-50s and a strong Torino would have certainly been able to challenge Real Madrid for early European domination. Unlike Manchester United, who after the Munich air disaster in 1958, found new fans from around the world, Torino only received a lot of sympathy. The club never recovered and has never come close to exerting such dominance.

One of the team's who stayed loyal to Torino after Superga were River Plate who even organised a prestigious friendly in the presence of Eva Peron a year later to raise funds for the families of the victims. Torino fielded a team with the heroes of that year - the likes of Boniperti, Gunnar Nordhal and Karl Hansen. Even today, Torino's second strip is often based on the famous River Plate 'Red Stripe', and the Argentine team in turn have a Granata away kit.

President Novo somehow mustered the strength to create a team for the depressing 1949-50 season with the donations of the Italian sports council CONI, and finished in a miraculous sixth place before the club experienced an inconsistent and unsure decade. Novo was not on the flight to Superga and many have said he spent the rest of his life wishing he was, such was the personal weight of the tragedy.

The 1950s were a sad time with a slow recovery from Superga with a series of young teams understandably struggling to emerge from the wreckage of the disaster. Players like Horst Buhtz, Hans Jeppson and Juan Carlos Tacchi kept fans smiling and the team in the right half of the league.

The FIAT empire extended in the 1950s and 60s dominated by the Agnelli family, historic owners of the 'other team'. Predominantly, it were the Torino fans built the FIAT cars for Agnelli and the Superga tragedy and unique working environment further intensified their bond and solidification. The Filadelfia became the epicentre of the Superga recovery, a place that Toro fans could always associate with their great team and great dominance. A kind of Granata Abbey Road.

The team resisted in Serie A until 1959, when under its fifth new ownership after Novo resigned in 1953, the club plummeted to Serie B for the first time in its history. Even sadder was the change of name to Torino Talmone in 1956 due to a sponsorship deal, the first of its kind in Italy, and the move to the Stadio Comunale, near the Filadelfia, marking the end of a glorious era. The 'Fila' was retained as the club's headquarters and heart.

The club's finances were by now disastrous and like in the 1990s, Toro went through a succession of Presidents including Luigi Morando, Mario Rubatto, Angelo Filippone and even a consortium of four businessmen. The stay in the second division lasted just a year, and the 1960s saw the beginnings of a revival. On their return to the top division, Torino welcomed two famous British imports - Denis Law and Joe Baker. Both have passed into Toro folklore although few remember their exploits on the pitch, this despite Baker scoring the winner in a Turin derby.

The two Brits lasted just a season, even less than that, considering that in February 1962, after a whisky-fuelled night out, they lost control of their car along the road which runs beside the River Po. Fortunately, both players survived although injuries ensured their respective Torino careers didn't. A disappointment considering Law's potential and talent. A year later another Englishman, Gerry Hitchens, arrived and with more success. The forward stayed in Italy for a number of years and helped Torino to a Cup Final defeat against Atalanta, the first of many disappointments in that competition. That same year marked the arrival of a President and respected man who would reign for twenty largely successful years - Orfeo Pianelli.

Torino weren't short of heroes in the 1960s from Lido Vieri to Aldo Agroppi to Nello Fossati to Enzo Bearzot and even legendary coach Nereo Rocco[7]. However, one player was to represent the renaissance of Torino and the lift the post-Superga gloom - Gigi Meroni.

Having begun his career at Como and then played for Genoa, Meroni arrived at Torino in 1964, ready to be coached by Rocco. Mercurial, peculiar and a man of many guises, Meroni was something of a messiah for the Torino supporters. He was the atypical footballer, a teetotal George Best, who did things his own way and made the headlines for his extra football loves - art, The Beatles, poetry, fashion and a famous and public relationship with a married woman.

In the year which Meroni joined Torino he lost his mentor Beniamino Santos, his former Genoa coach who died in a car crash. Santos, a Brazilian, was not only fondly remembered by Meroni but by Toro. In the two post-Superga seasons Santos scored 41 goals in two seasons for Torino, and still holds the goal per game record ratio for the club.

Meroni didn't see football like his peers. He had a disinterest in tactics and was not obsessed with winning matches whilst boring the public. He was born to entertain and represented a more liberal, free and extravert generation. He helped Torino to reach the semi-finals of the Cup-Winners' Cup in 1965 before a defeat against 1860 Munich and yet another Cup Final defeat, this time against Roma. Meroni featured for Italy in their disappointing 1966 World Cup campaign and was set to

---

[7] Trieste-born Nereo Rocco is considered one of the greatest Italian football coaches, above all for his spell at Milan where he turned the Rossoneri into a great club, winning two titles and two European Cups. He was nicknamed 'El Paron' and practised a 'classic' Italian way of playing the game.

become an international regular although in the era which spawned Sandro Mazzola and Gianni Rivera this was not an easy task. Meroni's unwillingness to conform, his trendy look and carefree persona were unfairly tagged as unprofessional by some coaches.

Meroni continued to shine for Torino and in the summer of 1967 was courted by the Agnelli family and the black & white stripe shirted team from the other side of the city. Meroni's legendary status amongst Torino supporters was confirmed when he rebuffed the move whilst President Pianelli was understandably tempted by a significant offer for his prized asset. The fans said 'no' and won.

Meroni began the 1967-68 season in great form. However, fate would again deliver a stunning blow to Torino Calcio. On the 17th October 1967, Meroni produced a stunning performance in a 4-2 Toro home win against Sampdoria. That evening he met up with his close friend and team-mate Fabrizio Poletti. They agreed to meet at Meroni's flat on Corso Re Umberto, 53 for dinner. However, Meroni had to wait for his girlfriend, Cristina, to return home as she had left his set of keys with the custodian. Meroni phoned Cristina from a nearby bar who assured him she was on her way back home.

In the meantime Meroni and Poletti headed back across the road, crossing a fair distance from the nearest set of traffic lights whilst the heavy flow of traffic passed. Meroni moved out onto the road but seeing an oncoming vehicle pass he quickly took a step back. Tragically, in that moment a passing vehicle hit Poletti on the leg and Meroni at full impact who died instantly. He was just 24 years old.

The player nicknamed the Butterfly had been hit by a car driven by a massive Torino fan. His name was Attilio Romero, the man who would become President of the Torino team which ceased to exist in 2005. Even more eerily, Gigi Meroni shared the same name as the pilot at the wheel of the plane which perished at Superga. A twist of fate which could only conspire against Torino Calcio.

Meroni's death was a crushing blow for the generation of Torino fans who had witnessed Superga and believed in a revival, a tragedy for supporters who idolised Meroni as others did Marilyn Monroe and Che Guevara. Meroni was not only a footballer but an icon of his generation. For the record he played 122 times for Toro, scoring 25 times.

The week after his death, Torino crushed their city rivals 4-0, a record post-war derby victory. Alberto Carelli, the young man who inherited Meroni's No 7 shirt for the match, was poignantly on the score sheet. At the scene of Meroni's death lies a picture attached to a lamppost, and permanently decorated with flowers. A rather tepid tribute to the 'La farfalla granata - Granata butterfly'.

The season, fortunately, would end in triumph for Torino. The club marked its return to the upper echelons of the Italian game with a Coppa Italia final victory after finishing on top of the group system implemented at the time, and thanks to a famous 2-0 victory in the final game at Inter with goals from Fossati and Nestor Combin consequently securing European qualification.

The growth of the club at the end of 1960s paved the way for the club's most successful period post-Superga - the 1970s. It was an era which witnessed the rise of communism in Italy and the tense political climate saw groups of workers unite against employers and a series of strikes and unrest. Under these conditions, many FIAT workers naturally chose to pledge their allegiance to Torino, as a way of rebelling against their employer.

Pianelli proved himself a shrewd and popular President putting his faith in a series of young coaches and players. The club took another Italian Cup in 1971, under the guidance of Giancarlo Cadè, again after an intense final five-game group with all matches played in June. Torino and Milan shared top of the group and were forced to play-off a one-off match, Torino amazingly winning on a penalty shoot-out. Under the rules of the time, the shoot-out was not between only two teams but the two players nominated the best 'rigorista'. For the record Toro's Sergio Maddè beat the Bambino d'Oro of Italian football, Gianni Rivera, by five goals to three. Cadè was then surprisingly replaced by another one of Pianelli's inspired coaching appointments.

Gustavo Giagnoni, the enigmatic Sardinian, is fondly remembered as one of Torino's most charismatic and popular trainers. A year after the Cup Final success, Giagnoni took Toro to within a hair's breath of their first Scudetto post-Superga and Torino fans still look back despairingly to a match in Genoa against Sampdoria. Trailing 2-1 with six minutes to go Agroppi saw a header cleared from behind the line by Samp defender Marcello Lippi, although it was adjudged not to have crossed the line.

The referee's decision cost Toro a crucial point. Lippi would in the late 1990s curiously become on of the most successful ever **ve coaches.

Giagnoni's team contained elements like 'keeper Luciano Castellini, Claudio Sala, Roberto Mozzini and Paolino Pulici who would go on to help the team lift Lo Scudetto in 1976. After coming close on a number of occasions, Toro finally had the better of their city rivals who were confined to second place. The inspiration was another new coach, Gigi Radice, whose strong personality and modern pressing game made its mark on a club which by now was well-organised and a major player again in Italian football.

The symbols of the seventh and last title were Sala, captain Zaccarelli and the 'Gemelli di gol' - Pulici and Francesco Graziani. The strikeforce are rated as the greatest Italian club forward partnership of all-time scoring over 200 goals for the club between them and Pulici, three times winning the top scorer award.

The Torino of 1976 enjoyed an intense battle with their city rivals for the title, winning every home game until the deciding match against Cesena which was drawn 1-1 but the 'other team's' defeat at Perugia confined the title to Torino. Radice, in a Sir Alex Ferguson rage, refused to celebrate the title win because of his team's draw and failure to preserve their perfect home record. However, the city made up for his initial anger, with mayor Diego Novelli claiming the celebrations were more spectacular than those following the Liberation. Pulici & Graziani defined another era in the history of Torino Calcio and Italian football and remain symbols of the last truly great Torino side. The names of that team read like poetry to a different generation: Castellini, Santin, Salvadori, Patrizio Sala, Mozzini, Caporale, Claudio Sala, Pecci, Graziani, Zaccarelli, Pulici.

Just when Torino fans felt it safe to celebrate, tragedy struck again. Giorgio Ferrini, captain of the side for over a decade, a record-breaking 443 league appearances for the Granata and a player who would literally run through walls for the club, suddenly died at the age of 37. Ferrini had retired in 1975 but remained at the club in a coaching capacity and a tribute to his class was his refusal to accept a place on the substitutes bench to enjoy a few minutes of the Scudetto triumph, admitting 'the victory did not belong to me'. Ferrini suffered from a brain haemorrhage and just five months after witnessing his club win the title, he too like Mazzola and Meroni was mourned.

Torino enjoyed an even stronger campaign the year after the 1976 title win, taking 50 out of the 60 points on offer, but their city rivals were to go one point better and claim the title in an epic battle. That same year Torino's sole European Cup campaign ended at the hands of Borussia Monchengladbach. After losing the home leg 2-1, Toro battled for a 0-0 draw in Germany despite finishing with eight men against 11 and with Graziani in goal. By the end of 70s, messers Pulici and Graziani were reaching the end of their careers and Torino prepared to usher in an underachieving yet talented generation in the 1980s.

Torino fans often talk about the 'Ragazzi della Filadelfia', players who grew up as part of the club's youth policy at the mythical stadium which even after it ceased to be used in the 1960s became the club's headquarters and training centre until the early 1990s. Under the guidance of the legendary Sergio Vatta, the club launched names like Agroppi, Benito Carbone, Angelo Cereser, Roberto Cravero, Antonio Comi, Dino Baggio, Giuseppe Dossena, Ferrini, Fossati, Diego Fuser, Lentini, Poletti, Pulici, Rosario Rampanti, Christian Vieri, Lido Vieri and Zaccarelli.

Several of these players would make their debuts in the 1980s, which was another romantic but massively unfruitful decade for the club. Three Coppa Italia finals were squandered including one on penalties and another in extra-time. The perennial bridesmaids often finished in the top-five and in 1985 perhaps should have claimed the Scudetto, finishing four points behind the surprise winners Verona.

Sergio Rossi replaced Pianelli, who perhaps stayed longer than he wished, in 1984 as club President. Both men are remembered fondly and Rossi was responsible for bringing the Granata icon of the 1980s to the club in 1984. Classy Brazilian playmaker Leo Junior arrived in Italy at the age of 30 but would stay in Turin for three seasons and his composure and class illuminated many afternoons at the Comunale. Another key element was striker Aldo Serena who was thought of fondly until he crossed the city and later went on to international fame. World Cup winning midfielder Beppe Dossena was another icon of this era.

The greatest moment of this decade was unquestionably a fantastic derby win over Michel Platini, Zibi Boniek et all in March 1983. Trailing 2-0 at half-time, Torino came back early in the second-half scoring via Dossena, Alessandro Bonesso and Fortunato Torrisi. Three goals in three minutes and an epic victory ensured. A less appreciated derby was a play-off for a UEFA Cup place in 1988 which the local rivals won on a penalty shoot-out.

Torino struggled in the late 1980s and under the helm of Rossi's successor, Massimo Gerbi, were relegated to Serie B in 1989 for the first-time since the 1950s, despite having a more than competitive team and interesting foreign investments like Luis Muller and Haris Skoro.

Despite the club's dwindling fortunes, the youth policy was about to enjoy its glory years with a number of national victories. Another positive factor was that season ticket sales were consistently over 20,000 and over 30,000 averaged the following year's Serie B games. In the last year before the Comunale closed to be replaced by the newly designed Stadio Delle Alpi, Eugenio Fascetti took Torino to the second division title thanks to a young team bleeding in the likes of Lentini, Gianluca Sordo, Cravero and Giorgio Venturin. However, the popular Fascetti was replaced for the forthcoming Serie A campaign by Emiliano Mondonico, who would be associated with Torino's better moments in the 1990s.

Had it not be for a mighty Milan side constructed by Silvio Berlusconi, Torino probably would have become champions of Italy in the early 1990s. Mondonico constructed a powerful side which finally gave the team a reputation in Europe and supremacy over the black & white striped team that suffered something of a slump.

Mondonico was initially bankrolled by Gianmarco Borsano, something of a saviour for the club having replaced Gerbi in 1989, and who invested heavily on new talent. Foreign stars like the Spaniard Rafael Martin-Vazquez, the Belgian Enzo Scifo and giant Brazilian Walter Casagrande proved shrewd investments and were united with three players whose commitment to the shirt went beyond total - Enrico 'Tarzan' Annoni, Roberto 'Rambo' Policano and Pasquale 'The Animal' Bruno. Three players who formed the spirit of the side whilst not retaining a close relationship with the match officials. Three players whose presence physiologically disturbed opposition strikers. On one famous occasion Bruno was alleged to have told Brescia's Romanian striker Florin Raducioiu that he would shoot him as the teams walked out for a match.

Venturin, Cravero and Luca Fusi provided the team with a touch of class, 'keeper Luca Marchegiani became the most expensive of the world when sold to Lazio in 1993 and added with the flair of Lentini, this was a strong and dynamic side.

In their first season back in the top flight, Torino qualified for the UEFA Cup. A year later, in the 1991-92 season, Toro finished second to Milan and embarked on their European adventure. That UEFA campaign became the latest unfortunate chapter in the club's history. The competition at that time was regularly stronger than the European Cup by nature of having more teams from stronger leagues, often those challenging for the league title, and that year Liverpool, Ajax and Real Madrid featured in the latter stages.

Toro defeated Reykjavik, Boavista, AEK Athens and BK Copenhagen before setting up a legendary semi-final against Real. The Granata were not overawed by a trip to Madrid and even took the lead in the Bernabeau before surrendering two late goals, but they had shown enough quality to begin the second leg with some hope.

A record crowd filled the Delle Alpi for the return leg and provided Toro with one of the greatest nights in the club's history. Lentini dribbled and dazzled and forced Ricardo Rocha into an eighth minute own goal, levelling the tie. Toro controlled the game thanks to Mondonico's tactical nous and defensive shell. The best efforts fell the home team's way and fifteen minutes from time a fantastic result was complete when Fusi slid in the side's second goal. The Granata won 3-2 on aggregate and set-up a final against an emerging Ajax side.

At that time Ajax, were beginning to bear the fruits of their legendary youth policy with the likes of Edwin van der Sar, Wim Jonk, Aron Winter, Brian Roy and Dennis Bergkamp coming through. Another full-house awaited Torino for the first-leg of the final. Two Casagrande goals were levelled out by two away goals including one from an impossible distance by Jonk - all to do in the second leg.

That night in Amsterdam is one of the last great nights in the club's history. And one of the most unfortunate. The game finished 0-0 and consequently Ajax won on away goals but not before Toro hit the woodwork three times including Sordo's near perfect header which rebounded off the crossbar three minutes from time. 'Il palo di Sordo' has become part of Torino folklore, and the match against Ajax has so many memories that people forget that Toro didn't come away with the cup. The classic and glorious defeat is epitomised by the famous image of Mondonico launching a chair onto the pitch in anger.

That summer President Borsano revealed his other face to the club's supporters and having invested in the team began selling large parts of it having used the club to gain the political power he craved. His ownership and initial successful running of the club had launched his own public profile and he began cashing back in on some of his investments. Cravero, Silviano Benedetti and Policano were sold. But the biggest uproar was for the sale of Lentini.

The localboy, the shy winger and symbol of the new Torino left for Milan for a then world record fee. Riots broke out on the streets of Turin, even if the price as hindsight would clarify, was more than fair. Milan deny eventually paying that much and in any case, Torino never saw the money, it went straight into Borsano's pockets and he left the club almost immediately after. Lentini's career never really took off after leaving Torino. After a relatively successful first-year at Milan he suffered a horrendous car crash the following summer, spent days in a coma, and his career afterwards was never the same. Another Torino talent wasted.

The team remained competitive for a few seasons and continued to enjoy European adventures but the spiralling debts left by Borsano would have their impact, were not successfully managed and the club's inevitable decline began. Initially the side remained competitive and the problems were ignored. In the 1992-93 campaign with Mondonico still at the helm, the side won the Italian Cup after an incredible final against Roma.

Having won the derby in the semi-final, Toro trounced Roma 3-0 in the first leg of the final and went to the capital in confident mood for the second-leg. However, the curse of Torino and Amsterdam a year earlier nearly resurfaced its ugly head again. An awful referring performance by Lorenzo Sguizzato, in charge of his last ever game, conceded Roma three dubious penalties and with half an hour to go, Torino were 5-2 down. It seemed Sguizzato was after a bonus retirement present. After the longest half-an-hour in the club's history and continuous Roma pressure, the Granata shirts resisted and claimed their last major trophy to date. Another fine case of doing things the hard way.

That summer, Marchegiani, Scifo and Carlos Aguilera were sold. Gradually, all elements of the side constructed in the early 1990s were being dismantled and not replaced adequately. The club received good money for some of these players but the money was not reinvested in the team.

Thanks to the goals of the lanky Andrea Silenzi, Torino remained competitive the following season and flirted again in Europe before a defeat in a dire match against Arsenal, watched from the stands by one Osama Bin Laden. Silenzi lost form and was overshadowed the following year by Ruggiero Rizzitelli, the hero of a double derby win, 3-2 and then 2-1 with Rizzi-gol scoring four goals between the two fixtures. Foreign stars such as Enzo Francescoli, Jocelyn Angloma and Abedi Pelè also offered moments of relief in these transition years.

Borsano was replaced at the helm by the young and ambitious Roberto Goveani. However, Goveani proved naive and irresponsible, immersing the club in further debt and to the point of bankruptcy. He was at the helm during the Coppa Italia success but his stay would be a short one and he would later spend time in prison for fraud. Only thanks to the intervention of Gianmarco Calleri, ex-President of Lazio, in 1994 and also due to some 'help' from FIGC President Luciano Nizzola, the club miraculously survived the summer of 1994 when it seemed they would be declared dead. For many reasons, bankruptcy then and not in 2005 may have been a blessing in disguise.

Calleri, a man who would not even stop at selling the chairs in the club's headquarters to save money, could do little to hide the club's problems. The youth team was stripped bare and its last major talent Christian Vieri was allowed to leave in exchange for a veteran Venezia player. Putting that error into context, Vieri has since commanded over 130 million euros in transfer fees. Attendances fell, the club plummeted down the league and gained little in sponsorship or external money. The club suffered a horrendous 1995-96 season, despite having what seemed a relatively competitive team, and slipped down to Serie B. Since when Torino Calcio have been as stable as a young child with an ice-cream on a sea-saw.

The first season back in the lower division was one of the most monotonous in the side's history with average players such as Carmine Nunziata, Valeriano Fiorin and mysterious foreigners such as Samuel

Ipoua donning the shirt once reserved for Mazzola, Meroni and Pulici. The side under young Coach Mauro Sandreani finished ninth. Calleri, the apparent saviour of the club, was relieved of the owernership in 1997 by a Genoa based consortium, headed by Massimo Vidulich, young and with bright ideas. They brought in Graeme Souness as Coach and bankrolled the return of Lentini.

Souness proved a misguided appointment in the battling world of Serie B and the players struggled to understand his instructions and the team began the campaign in dire straits. Souness left after six matches and once Edoardo Reja got to grips with the team and introduced some wise signings, the side flew. However, the slow start and injuries towards the end of the season weighed and the club eventually lost that famous play-off with Perugia.

Reja, despite his popularity and decent brand of football (a rare thing in the last ten years) was replaced by the return of Mondonico who reunited with a chunkier and slower Lentini and thanks to the goals of Marco Ferrante took the team back up to the top-flight.

Mondonico, though, had become more prudent and conservative in his old age and struggled badly once back in Serie A, baptising some young players too late in the season and playing for the draw or even defeat too often. After initially spending modestly, the new regime were also immersed in financial problems and made cut-backs in areas where had they invested the club could have blossomed. The continual dismantling of the youth team was evidence of this. The Genovese consortium grew tired of their expensive and dwindling investment and in April 2000, as the team were faced with relegation to Serie B the club was sold to Signor Franco Cimminelli.

Chapter 3 - Cimmi & Tilli: The men who killed Torino Calcio

Franco Cimminelli, a man with a permanently smug and self-satisfied smile, is without question the most contested President in the history of Torino Calcio and fully deserves his classification as the worst.

Albeit at the beginning of Cimminelli's reign being rid of the Genovese consortium who had promised much, invested badly and left heavier debts was no bad thing. The problem was that from the start Cimminelli was about as a disastrous candidate for ownership the club as possible.

In April 2000, Cimminelli inherited a club Serie B-bound with a large and ageing squad, a spiralling debt, dwindling attendances and meagre sponsorship or income. Torino played in an enormous, unpopular grey stadium owned by the council that was a financial burden rather than a source of profit. The club was frozen in the past and unable to follow the ever-changing speed of modern football. Apathy amongst club employees and fans ruled. Spectacularly, Cimminelli would leave the helm in a worse state.

Cimminelli hails from Crotone, Calabria. This alone, had it not been for his other succession of failings, could have been accepted. However, Cimminelli's southern roots coupled with his carefree arrogance caused an immediate climate of suspicion. Italians feel very attached to their 'bell tower', the place they come from, feeling a greater sense of belonging to their home town and their roots rather than their country which is understandable considering the way the country was 'unified' and how it still remains fractionised. The great Torino Presidents had been Piedmontese or even better Torinese. Cimminelli might have made his money in Piedmont but could never be Piedmontese. In fact, to be classified a genuine Piedmontese, its necessary to trace ancestry back seven generations. There is still an inverted snobbery from some northerners towards southerners, particularly in a city like Turin, which saw the rapid influx of immigrations from the south in the 1950s and 60s. However, the early anti-Cimminelli feeling wasn't simply misplaced racism.

Cimminelli's arrogance and bickering during his takeover bid for the club, which dragged on an on through the early months of the year 2000, put him off on a bad footing with the press and the fans. Some observers feel that his aggressive methods and ill-timed comments during his acquisition for the club even contributed to the team's relegation that year. He had publicly stated that he would replace the entire backroom and playing staff - not what a team battling against the drop needed to hear.

After buying Toro, Cimmi boasted: "From what I have spent to buy the club and pay of some of the debts, I could fill a room with cheques." Cimminelli is a form of Ebenezer Scrooge who on the rare occasions that he dips his hand in his pocket, lets everybody know, compensating by neglecting to pay some of his more pending financial obligations.

His plastics company Ergom, which he formed in the 1970s, and which had grown within 20 years to employ 3,000 people and become a significant supplier to the motor industry was almost part of the FIAT group. Therefore, he is practically in the pockets of the company which controlled ***entus. He was a supporter of the 'other team', having been witnessed celebrating one of their rare victories in Europe. His footballing knowledge was minimal and interest of the game even more scarce. He wasn't rich enough to make the club great and not prepared to spend big. He knew little and cared less about the club's glorious history, repeatedly pronouncing names of former players wrongly.

Cimminelli appointed Beppe Aghemo, at least a Torino supporter, as his first President although the relationship lasted barely a few months. It was Aghemo who convinced Cimminelli to buy the club, being a close friend and business partner. Aghemo saw the potential behind the reconstruction of the Filadelfia and the Comunale, the latter stadium having been earmarked for renovation when Turin was given the Host City contract in 1999 for the Olympic Winter Games.

However, the pair disagreed about the appointment of personnel for the following Serie B campaign and Cimminelli also grew tired of what he considered Aghemo's rash and popularistic statements and rhetoric.

Cimminelli famously commented: "He (Aghemo) always speaks about Superga but those stupid Torino supporters should stop climbing the hill and crying about the past."

Cimminelli wanted to appoint veteran Carlo Mazzone as Coach and Enrico Pieroni as Director General. Deals had been agreed with both. However, Pieroni's potential appointment caused an uproar amongst Toro fans due to his association with Perugia, the ill-fated playoff final in 1998, and for an incident during the 1999-00 campaign when he got into an argument with Torino goalkeeper Luca Bucci and ended it with having a cigarette stubbed out his face (Italian 'keepers are still partial to tobacco).

Cimminelli replaced the nostalgic and misguided Aghemo with one of his old associates, Attilio 'Tilli' Romero. His name initially meant little to Torino supporters until it was revealed that tragically it was Romero behind the wheel which killed the unfortunate Meroni. Whether Romero saw the opportunity to take the Presidency as a means for making amends for the tragedy remains to be seen (although an urban myth and it remains just that says that Romero was not behind the wheel of that car, but he was the passenger and was covering for somebody else, whose life would have been scarred by the affair). Whatever the truth, and urban myths often remain that, Romero's appointment was certainly a precarious one.

Romero's background was also tied to FIAT, having worked as Head Press Officer and chief spokesperson for Agnelli. The fans considered this a life spent working for the 'enemy'. Romero was a contested appointment due not only to the Meroni affair but his tragic appearance. Quite simply one of the ugliest men ever to walk the face of the earth, Romero with his long saggy face, Penfold glasses, unkept mane of hair with an ever widening bald spot, looked like the unfortunate cousin of Inter President Massimo Moratti. He was not a man who inspired confidence.

It seemed a deeply precarious and emotional step. Romero is a Torino fan and a man who had a passionate feeling for the club. However, his level of expertise at guiding a club of Torino's stature was negligible and the story regarding Meroni was beyond to paralyse him should things gone wrong. Romero's role, though, was never as a decision maker, he was the fall-gay for Cimminelli, the Fredo Corleone of the family. The few decisions which were made during Cimminelli's five-year reign were made by the patron, the scarce regard for personnel and poor planning stemmed from the owner. The first-team responsibilities were undertaken by the director generals, who in certain cases, were perhaps given too much freedom not only by Cimminelli but by Romero.

Whether Romero was appointed because he could fill such a transparent role or whether he enjoyed neglecting responsibilities is debatable. He seldomly challenged Cimminelli, and seemed to pass his time in endless Lega Calcio meetings, although he was rarely a President who made his mark made. Men like Cagliari's Massimo Cellino, Paolo De Luca of Siena and Perugia's Luciano Gaucci, in charge of smaller clubs always made their presence more noted. The only time it can be said that Romero stood up and was counted was during the Catania affair, when in the summer of 2003, Serie B was stupidly and unnecessarily expanded.

Romero retained good ties with the Agnelli family and the fans were understandably worried about external influence over the club. The Toro relationship with the Agnelli family, however, has not always been as undignified and as bitter as that with their team. The Agnelli's and Giovanni Agnelli Snr, after all, helped keep the heroes of Superga in jobs during the Second World War, contributing to the fact that the players stayed together afterwards and continued to train. With the collaboration of Novo, a team comprising some Bianconeri players but predominantly those of Il Grande Torino were kept together for the 1944 war time championship. Giovanni's son and namesake, the most famous Agnelli, and not only for his legendary playboy antics, had respect for the Granata admitting a derby was the game, "I least like to win and least like to lose." His brother, Umberto, had a more hostile feeling to Toro.

The cross-city rival in Turin is a complicated one and not only because it's not a genuine cross-city clash. The black and white side, are not a significant presence all things considered, despite their mass trophy cabinet, undoubted popularity throughout the country and zealous marketing campaigns. Turin is the city of Torino. The Bianconeri have no spiritual home (The Filadelfia), no community (the Mirafiori area), no famous bars (The Sweet) or no place of worship (Superga).

Their supporters, without generalising, are formed from the southern immigrants of the 1950s and 1960s, most of whom traditionally follow **ve or Inter, partial followers of football, gloryhunters, Miss Italia winners, the Agnelli family, Flavio Briatore-types and millions of supporters from small towns or areas around Italy with no catchment base or major club. They rarely fill their stadium, despite being the most supported team in Italy and as Turin-based national sports daily *Tuttosport* in its electoral campaigns for the club would have you believe also in the world. Champions' League crowds can be as low as 5,000, Coppa Italia matches have hit less than 1,000 and for a misty Turin afternoon against Ascoli, no more than 21,000 people show up. Hardly passion.

There's an old saying which says that a supporter of ***ventus can become a supporter of Torino but never viceversa. People follow the former but worship the latter. Toro fans know fate has been less kind to them, that they will always live in the shadow of their more stylish and designer label neighbours but will never be defeated on pride, passion nor history. Supporting **ve is like buying a Eros Ramazzotti cd, brash and popular, supporting Torino like owning a Chet Baker lp, nostalgic, tragic and romantic.

What's more, throughout Italy, the Bianconeri are not considered a pleasant club with their historical favouring from referees, drug links in the late 1990s, and omnipresence at the head of the Italian game. In equal measure, they are more than respected for managing a budget successfully, their self-financing philosophy and resilience on the field which is perhaps the only comparison between the two clubs. It's not surprising that amongst Torino heroes are players who have never played for the club. Johnny Rep, Felix Magath, Renato Curi, Karl-Heinz Reidle, Alessandro Calori and Predrag Mijatovic are all players who have scored famous goals against **ve consigning themselves unknowingly to Torino folklore.

On the field, the stakes have always been tight, despite the disparity in the number of titles won. However, in recent years Torino's demise has led the way for the black and whites to build a slight advantage. The last Torino success was a double one in 1994-95, perhaps too much to ask, having been followed by a long and depressing drought. A year later, **ve inflected a 5-0 victory at the hands of a weak Torino side, a few seasons after came a 4-0 loss and a recent derby saw Torino finish with eight men and but almost grabbing a remarkable point only for defender Stefano Fattori to miss the most amazing open goal. In a season of calamity drama, that of the 2002-03 campaign, when the Granata finished rock bottom of Serie A, they still managed to find some passion in the derby.

The most remarkable recent derby since the famous March 1983 afternoon, when Torino scored three times in three minutes to win 3-2, came in October 2001, proving one of the few pleasant afternoons in Cimminelli's reign. Torino had just been promoted to Serie A and failed to win any of the opening six games of the season. A defeat against the enemy would have proved costly for popular Coach Giancarlo Camolese and at half-time it seemed Camolese may as well collect his belongings (a decision already popular with Cimminelli who detested Camolese from the moment he defied him the year earlier) with Torino outclassed and trailing 3-0.

However, two half-time substitutions changed the tide and goals from Cristiano Lucarelli and a Marco Ferrante penalty pulled it back to 3-2. More Torino pressure paid dividends and ten minutes from time Riccardo Maspero tapped home from close range. Maspero had already earnt hero status before the events of the final minutes of the match. A scuffle in the box saw the Bianconeri awarded their customary last minute penalty. Torino hearts sunk, aware that Lady Luck was with the La Vecchia Signora once again. As players argued with the referee, Maspero dug a hole with his boot on the penalty spot. Marcelo Salas put the ball down and amazingly smashed the penalty into orbit. Only later that night were television images clear in depicting Maspero's trick. For once Torino had pulled a fast one.

Camolese was unquestionably one of the few successful appointments during Cimminelli's area, and one of his cheapest, although his appointment was more by chance than design. Gigi Simoni had initially been appointed Coach, and at an expensive cost, for the side which began Cimmi's first campaign as owner in Serie B. As well as Simoni, Marco Ferrante who was always a guarantee of goals if not teamwork, was retained on an expensive contract as was playboy defender Fabio Galante whilst Diego De Ascentis became the club's record signing from Milan. Former international Bucci played in goal and Stefan Schwoch, a Serie B stalwart, spearheaded the attack with Ferrante. All in all it was a formidable team to play at the second division level and for perhaps the only time in his reign, Cimminelli spent considerably.

The team began badly and after eight games had never been so close in Serie C. Simoni, a Torino hero in the 1960s before he crossed the city, was appointed by Sandro Mazzola, son of Il Grande Torino captain Valentino, and Cimminelli's eventual choice as Director General instead of the contested Pieroni. Mazzola Jnr had trained with his father at the Filadelfia, although he was perhaps too young to cherish the memories. In 2000 he was in his late 50s and finally fulfilling a dream of working for his father's club having spent his playing career at Inter after being discarded by Torino as a youngster.

Mazzola was essentially in charge of the transfer operations and Cimminelli's first team budget, and he had previously appointed Simoni whilst enjoying the same role a few years previously at Inter, where with a massive transfer outlay they took the team led by Ronaldo to the UEFA Cup and a second-place league finish. At Torino, however, Simoni failed to unite the dressing room nor find any balance on the field and was an old, tired and predictable appointment. Following the stuttering start to the season, Simoni was sacked and replaced by the considerably cheaper option of youth team boss Camolese, a man Cimminelli claimed he didn't know the existence of only a few months earlier.

Mazzola's lack of expertise in the transfer market formed part of Toro's problems. He was a likeable if passive character, too generous with the players and proved a nostalgic but misguided appointment. He failed to attract good young players to the club nor had an eye for constructing a team, on the basis of a tactical or technical blueprint. He was not Erbstein. The foreign market was never exploited and when it was, Mazzola signed players like the toothless Swede Yksel Osmanovski. It was expected Mazzola would utilise his special relationship with Inter to bring some talented players on loan to Torino. However, apart from the forgotten Argentine Sixto Peralta, none arrived. Mazzola's most infamous signing was the hopeless Uruguayan international Federico Magallanes from Venezia who Romero bizarrely described as a mix between 'Meroni, Gento and Best...', a phrase sure to be etched on his gravestone.

Mazzola's foreign market legacy was millionaire signing Jose Franco, the leggy Uruguayan, who came to the conclusion of his extortionate contract in June 2005. A player who summed up the mismanagement of the early Cimminelli years. Toro paid up to seven million euros for a player who took six months to make his league debut because of injury problems and an international transfer which arrived embarrassingly late. Until the transfer arrived he was neglected by the club and forced to accept the hospitality of Paolo Montero, a Bianconeri defender.

When Franco did appear from the wilderness he injured his knee again before enjoying his best spell during an ill-fated three years on the River Po, scoring a couple of blistering goals as Toro secured survival in Serie A. However, the remaining three years of his contract proved to be a nightmare. In the following top-flight campaign, the ex-Penarol forward again suffered injury problems and barely featured. Following relegation, Franco featured in just 23 of Toro's 88 Serie B matches, failing to score and starting just four times. His limited technical ability was embarrassingly evident as were his enormous boat shaped feet. To his credit, he was a popular character in the dressing room. However, a seven million euro motivational speaker seemed a little excessive and months after the old club's demise, a weighty Franco was still seen walking the streets of Turin without a club.

Other millionaires under the Cimmi era enjoyed diverse fortunes. Striker Cristiano Lucarelli was signed for 7.5 million euros and expected to spearhead the Granata attack for a decade, offering the kind of target-man missed since Graziani left in 1981. Instead, Lucarelli stayed just for two years - one average, one nightmarish. The first year ended with a tally of nine goals including a famous winner against Milan. However, Lucarelli's form in front of goal dipped up as the season developed and his goal drought would continue five months into the following season.

He was one of few players to stand up to Cimminelli, once even throwing food at him during a club meal before another famous incident before an Intertoto Cup match in Austria. Travel arrangements had caused an almighty rift between the patron and the players. Lucarelli led the rebellion who wanted to travel to Austria by plane. Cimminelli insisted that they travelled by bus. The row ended with Cimminelli publicly called Lucarelli 'a dickhead,' a stimulus for Lucarelli's worst ever career in professional football and ending his association with the club.

In his second season, Lucarelli failed to punch is weight, he only gained it. The ever expansion of his gut was a sign of a depressed player who when entering the field was more likely to hit someone than trouble the opposition defence. Torino's season ended in desperate relegation - the club's worst ever Serie A campaign - and Lucarelli finished scoring just once - a goal from all of 2cm out.

When the team were relegated to Serie B, he negotiated a loan move to home town club Livorno, a club of which he was a self-confessed ultrà in order to cure his 'depression'. However, the move would revitalise Lucarelli and Livorno but not Toro. Lucarelli's first year in Tuscany ended with promotion to Serie A and over 30 league goals. In that same Serie B campaign, Toro languished in mid-table and in need of that fire-power.

Lucarelli had promised to return after just a year to fulfil his dream of be coming a Torino idol. That never materialised as Lucarelli declared: 'Or Livorno, or I retire'. The player took a massive pay cut and Toro eventually a 80% loss on their investment to allow him to move to Livorno. Since when he has become Serie A's top scorer and an international footballer. And one few examples of a footballer with some identification to the club for whom he plays. A few more Lucarelli's and Toro may have been better off following the fall of the club in August 2005.

Galante and Ferrante were two other player paid highly by Cimminelli. Galante, unloved and unwanted by Toro fans, was the atypical Torino player, a stylish playboy more likely to appear on the front of a woman's weekly than football weekly *Guerin Sportivo*. Ferrante, on the other hand, scored over 120 goals for the club (admittedly a lot of penalties) over nearly a decade but was to become ostracised by Cimminelli for the size of his contract.

Following Simoni's dismissal, Camolese himself risked the sack after a poor start which included amongst other results a shock 2-1 defeat at little Cittadella. However, just before Christmas, Camolese began to find a winning formula, with a three-man defence, five-man midfield and merciless attack which generally created one opportunity a game and took it. Either side of New Year, and with the prima donna Ferrante loaned to Inter, he led the team to eight straight victories, becoming the springboard for Toro to launch a record-breaking Serie B campaign, winning virtually every game until the end of the season, most by a 1-0 scoreline. Camolese even publicly defied Cimminelli when famously playing Mauro Bonomi, a defender Cimminelli wanted rid of due to his expensive contract, fielding him in a 2-0 win over Cagliari hours after

Cimminelli said he would never play for the club again. That was effectively the moment Camolese signed his own dismissal.

"We won the league on the field and also won on the balance sheets," claimed Cimminelli after promotion to Serie A, promising the club would never return back to Serie B and lauding the club's financial 'improvement.' The following season with the addition of Lucarelli, Camolese repeated similar tactics in Serie A and had it not been for an insipid final two months of the campaign the team may have qualified for Europe directly, which considering the strength of the side would have been an incredible achievement.

That first season back in Serie A wasn't though without its drama. In March, with the team just a matter of points away from survival, controversy blew up after a debated 1-1 home draw with Bologna. Torino had taken the lead before the Rossoblu equalised for a draw which suited both teams, although the result was not paramount in either of the team's eventual destiny. Days after the game, television images revealed a discussion between Toro defenders Galante and Daniele Delli Carri just before a Bologna corner. Lip-readers claimed Galante said to Delli Carri "(non) dobbiamo fargli fare gol - we must (or musn't) let them score." Bologna promptly scored from the corner. The players protested their innocence saying it the 'non' part of Galante's phrase was not picked up clearly by lip-readers. The drama passed after a few days but suspicions over that game haven't.

As it was, the team qualified for the summer-long Intertoto Cup, a competition which would cause Torino to enter the forthcoming Serie A season beset with problems due to the Lucarelli incident before the trip to face Austrian side FC Bregenz. The team scraped through the first round to face a clash against Spanish side Villarreal. Lucarelli was sent-off in Spain as Torino lost the next round on penalties despite winning the first leg 2-0. The season brought one disaster after another. Lucarelli was again dismissed in a 6-0 defeat at Milan after he reacted to Milan's showboating. The team lost their first four matches of the season. Camolese was sacked after the team's first league win over the season because of a subsequent Coppa Italia defeat at home to Empoli. Another Torino and Cimminelli record - sacking a coach after a league victory!

Camolese had created a united dressing room, with a group of players albeit overpaid by Cimminelli and Mazzola but who had apart from a bad start to the 2002-03 season delivered results and had an effective if mundane way of playing. The strong dressing room bond was also in a strange way thanks to Cimminelli as almost everyone was united against him. The success of his team had also convinced Cimminelli not to spend any more money, as the patron overestimated the strength of the team in advance of the 2002-03 season.

The reaction of the players to Camolese's dismissal was understandably negative but the atmosphere worsened by the appointment of 'lefty' Renzo 'Red' Ulivieri as Coach. Ulivieri was unanimously detested by the players and the fans, his public stripping of the team in front of journalists after a 4-0 derby humiliation hardly helped. He barely won a game and his reign culminated in a depressing 3-0 home defeat by Milan which was abandoned when Torino fans invaded he pitch to protest against the team. The club were banned from the Stadio Delle Alpi for the remainder of the campaign and were effectively relegated by January. It was also the cue for Ulivieri and Mazzola to leave the club, the former universally despised, the latter disillusioned by the way things had gone. Ulivieri, like Simoni before him, was replaced by a youth team boss in Toro stalwart Giacomo Ferri. Other heroes from the past stepped into Mazzola's shoes with Cravero and Zaccarelli appointed in technical positions. Cimminelli had a common way of appeasing supporters by appointing and then ruining ex-heroes in key strategic positions.

On the after day the team were relegated to Serie B, playing their 'home match' against Udinese at the neutral venue of Reggio Emilia, 50,000 Torino fans 'celebrated' the relegation, curiously enough on the 4th May - the anniversary of the Superga disaster. 'La giornata del orgoglio granata' was a major success in uniting Torino supporters in a common faith, both in a desire to protect and maintain the club's values but also to unite against Cimminelli. The march started at the Fila, passed Meroni's memorial, many of the 'stupid idiots' made the trip to Superga where ex-players made emotional speeches, before the day finished in Piazza San Carlo, with scenes which to an outsider seemed as if Torino had won the title. 'La nostra fede non retrocede - Our faith is not relegated' read the most poignant banner.

From that moment on, Cimminelli who had spent money very badly, stopped spending and only moaned about how much he had invested. Players like Lucarelli, Franco, Ferrante, Galante, Bucci and De Ascentis earned high salaries and they became crippling once the team's league placement failed to match its ambition. The team's two best players - Ferrante and Lucarelli - never gelled on or off the pitch and it was the younger, more promising but emotional Lucarelli who made way.

Cimminelli's arrogance and Romero's lack of character shaped these years. Both may have been forgiven had they actually shown respect for the fans but Cimminelli's infamous ridiculing of the 'idiots' who visit Superga to remember Il Grande Torino effectively ended his already icy rapport with the fans before it began. The appointment of his 21-year old and 21-stone son Simone, as vice-President was an object of ridicule. Cimmi Jnr became infamous for various acts of drunken behaviour. Cimmi's wife, Signora Franca Cimminelli was mocked for her pottery exhibitions which she hosted across the city.

Cimminelli soon grew tired of his investment but despite his famous 'I'll sell the club for a euro,' declaration never really came close to giving it up. Either because his intentions to sell were never serious or because nobody serious moved forward. The most public bid for the club came from the Latvian Aleksandrs Basharin, whose bid to take over the club dominated the papers for much of the spring of 2003, although Cimminelli eventually laughed it off as some bad publicity. He claimed that Basharin never offered the guarantees necessary and most significantly that he and Romero would not 'give in' to the first person to make an offer.

The legacy of Cimminelli and Romero is a spectacular one. They took the club to its lowest ever Serie A position, a year later to its lowest Serie B standing with another ex-hero Ezio Rossi as coach. They took the team into Europe and then as quickly out again, went through four coaches alone in the 2002-03 season, never made any visit to the Torino museum at Superga and indeed became the first Torino team to be asked not to attend the service in 2004. They refused to extend the contract of the popular nor expensive captain Antonino Asta who during the 2001-02 became the last Torino player to feature for the Italian national team. They hung onto the club possessively despite claims almost from the outset that he wanted to sell it. They witnessed some of the club's lowest ever attendances and caused the Curva Maratona to go on strike during the end of the 2003-04 campaign. But for a miracle the Stadio Filadelfia didn't become a supermarket. Cimminelli invested in a youth team in Congo promising to set up a Torino school in Africa, but the project lasted just months. He owned a Serie C club, Lecco, which was to act as a feeder side for Torino. It went bust, immersed in debts as did another club he controlled, Moncalieri, in the Turin hinterland. But still, Cimminelli didn't learn his lesson.

Cimminelli's arrogance meant that few players respected him or believed his promises. His stubbornness and lack of expertise saw the departure of Camolese, a man who was probably capable of keeping the team afloat in Serie A. His arrogance continued to upset Torino supporters, and his arrogance would ultimately desert him.

Cimminelli was so confident of Serie A football that he celebrated the play-off success against Perugia under the shower with the players. He clearly knew the extent of the club's debt, that he had done little to resolve it, and that the club's chances of playing in Serie A were under threat. Romero never had the courage nor power to speak up, instead continued to spread ridiculous statements and messages.

Cimminelli had banked everything on what proved to be a false guarantee signed by a broker called Beppe Gallo, who mysteriously enough was embroiled in the Venezia and Genoa affair, another negative story which was to dominate the Italian football skyline during the summer of 2005. Within days of Cimminelli's guarantee being declared false, the police had raided the club's headquarters and the situation was declared desperate and terminal.

In turned out that Cimminelli had not paid a large part of the club's taxes in five years, the players had not been played for fourth months (although payment of club officials was on time) and that the club's debt stood at 51 million euros. On top of this there was a stadium to finish building, a team to mould for Serie A, and the minor fact that he had missed the deadline to deposit the guarantee the club's place in Serie A. But the rules mattered little to a man like Cimminelli - a man who had broken all negative records whilst in charge of Torino and a man capable of destroying the club, a club eighteen months away from its one hundredth birthday.

Chapter 4 - Protests & Marches but no cheque

The bid to save the club was led on various fronts. Cimminelli, with that permanently frozen grin, began contacting banks, assurance agencies, brokers, Sky television, his nephew's piggy bank any possible avenue to find some, part or all of the money needed to enable the club to take its place in the top division. No club had ever been denied promotion due to their finances not being in place, Cimminelli had banked on Serie A football and the subsequent sponsorship and television benefits to enable the club to reduce some of its crippling debt.

Cimminelli's shadow, Romero, when not absent was his usual annoying self, making vain, empty or ridiculous comments like 'we have a Champions' League budget,' 'we will register for Serie A without any trouble', reassuring the players that they would be able to honour the Serie A place which was rightfully claimed on the field of play.

Sergio Chiamparino, the mayor of Turin and Torino supporter, worked on two fronts, trying as much as he could, as much as anyone could, to help Cimminelli find an ally or a loan. On the other front, the mayor was well aware that a contingency plan was needed. He began contacting entrepreneurs willing enough to supply the necessary funds for a Lodo Petrucci, a clause created by Gianni Petrucci[8], which offered teams faced with bankruptcy the opportunity to restart under a different name, but without their honours, assets and most importantly debts. The carrot was the opportunity to restart from the division immediately below than the one they were initially registered in, providing a certain amount of capital was guaranteed.

Therefore, should Torino go bust and a Lodo was authorised then there was the option of Serie B. Failing that the option was to restart in Serie

---

[8] Gianni Petrucci is the head of the Italian National Olympic Committee (Comitato Olimpico Nazionale Italiano - CONI).

C2A, effectively the fourth division, which remains at an amateur rather than professional footing. Recent giants to go broke include Fiorentina and Napoli.

Fiorentina went bust due to debts mounted by former owner Vittorio Cecchi Gori and were dispatched to Serie C2 following relegation from Serie A to B. The Tuscan club made a rapid rise through the divisions. Thanks to Diego Della Valle[9], they escaped Serie C2 and were promoted to Serie C1 immediately. Then in the mess which immersed Italian football in the summer of 2003, with the expansion of the top two divisions, Fiorentina were promoted to Serie B on 'sporting merit'. This was a contested decision in many quarters, and considered almost immoral, but seemed a way of the FA appeasing the side for the heavy punishment of being relegated two divisions just a year earlier. Fiorentina then gained promotion to Serie A despite finishing sixth in Serie B, winning a play-off against Perugia.

Napoli, immersed in debt after a horrific post-Maradona decade, benefited from the Lodo Petrucci, finishing in Serie C1 and under a new owner, Aurelio De Laurentis[10], began to rebuild albeit from humbler roots.

Few Torino fans, fresh from having witnessed the side battle so dramatically back to Serie A wanted to think about Serie B football again. The long special night against Perugia, the sufferance of the play-offs and the sweet nature of the victory was fresh in people's minds and couldn't be deemed worthless. Serie B is a tough league to get out of, and one which offers a poor spectacle for supporters. The general standard of football is average with most teams on an even footing. It's far more physical and cynical than the top division and not a league where the most skilled teams always prevail. What's more a big club, like Torino, can always guarantee meeting opponents playing 110%. This bright, young team had some semblance of future and pride even if with Cimminelli in charge, its potential would be rather limited.

A few local journalists, and the *La Stampa* newspaper in particular, saw the opportunity as a perfect chance to be rid of the hated Cimminelli and

---

[9] Diego Della Valle is owner of one of Italy's biggest shoe empires.

[10] Aurelio De Laurentis, one of Italy's most prominent film producers, took over Napoli in September 2004.

to start afresh even if it be in Serie B. After spending so much of the last decade in the second division would another year really matter? and would the club under Cimmi have the foundations to rebuild itself in Serie A? or would the continue yo-yoing between the two divisions further crippling the club's already precarious financial standing? And Chiamparino, seemingly losing patience with Cimminelli, was finding supporters of the Lodo Petrucci route, but moral support rather than financial.

The month of July would be a major battle between the three major newspapers covering Torino. *Tuttosport*, often derogatively referred to as TuttoJu** or Tuttoballe due to its massive coverage of Italy's most popular team™ and ridiculous transfer rumours which even under the Cimminelli era saw players like Michael Owen and Ryan Giggs linked with the Granata. It's a newspaper which covers primarily football, even the 2006 Winter Olympics are rarely afforded a mention.

Six pages are usually guaranteed for SuperJu**, the greatest team the world has ever seen and winner of as many European Cups as Nottingham Forest - one awarded after the Heysel stadium disaster, the other following a penalty shoot-out in their home country. The newspaper often seems like an electoral publication for the black and white side, such is the propaganda and vitriolic headlines it produces.

Milan and Inter get a page each, the other Serie A teams are covered sparingly, whilst Torino are usually relegated to pages 12-14, before a significant space for local football. It is however a newspaper, which has a positive tone, at the sake of being unbelievable, has also strove to maintain and fight for justice on behalf of Toro and has always been anti-Cimminelli. However, *Tuttosport*, at least for the initial part of the month were guilty of swallowing some of Cimminelli's promises which stretched from the sublime to the ridiculous.

La Stampa, on the other hand, was cold and pessimistic. Already in early July, they printed a photo on its front cover which would be repeated on the day Torino temporarily perished. It was an image taken last season of Marazzina lying on his back in despair after missing a goal. *La Stampa* wrote off Cimminelli as soon as the news of the fraud broke out (but still at the price of nine euros offered a DVD of Torino's promotion with Cimminelli celebrating under the shower whilst a scraggy Romero was interviewed with the mayor at his shoulder).

La Stampa bleakly pointed to an immediate future in Serie C2 as often as they did Serie B, sighting even the difficulties in finding someone to sanction a Lodo Petrucci. A club with a million supporters, located in a city about to host the Olympic Winter Games and with a deep history, was struggling to find sponsors or support. Something which reflected rather badly on the Torinese high society and industrialists. Maybe the difficulties which faced Calleri, Goveani, Vidulich and Cimminelli put people off. Maybe nobody wanted to move forward whilst the club was still not theoretically 'free of charge'. Maybe the power of the city's other team was too overwhelming. Maybe the city of Turin lacks a heart. Its people certainly don't. *La Stampa*'s editorials, often written by the excellent Massimo Gramellini and evergreen Toro writer Gianpaolo Ormezzano pointed to a new beginning even in if Serie B. An interview with Pinga promising he would stay in Serie B with Torino was published and at no point in July did Turin's principal newspaper seem to even consider the option that the team could play in the top-flight.

La Gazzetta Dello Sport adopted the more partial and realistic stance of the three. Its tone always that of a newspaper without a vested interested. There were days when the news seemed less negative than others, even days when Torino were not even mentioned (there was after all other teams embroiled in a similar mess from Messina to Reggina, from Perugia to Salernitana, transfers to report, the Genoa match fixing scandal and the protests of teams claiming the right to be reinstated in various divisions because of others financial neglection).

The other newspapers didn't deny space to the Torino affair. *La Repubblica*, Milan-based, adopted a slightly tamer version of La Stampa's stance, the third daily sportspaper, the Rome-based, *Corriere Dello Sport*, barely covers Torino due to the fact that *Tuttosport* is the Turin-based and *La Gazzetta* also offers ample coverage. *Torino Cronica*, a sort of local tabloid newspaper, was vociferously anti-Cimminelli.

Only during the first few days of July following the promotion to Serie A was promotion mentioned, and indeed a new Coach appointed. Daniele Arrigoni, a man with a geography teacher's fringe and fresh from inspiring Cagliari to Serie A survival, took the helm despite the fears that he may not eventually have a job within a month. The mood within the squad was still falsely positive. Zaccarelli was alone running some semblance of a club and following assurances from Cimminelli and Romero, was able at least to convince the players that everything would be fine. The club split into two halves - Zaccarelli and the players, Cimminelli and Romero.

A Danish player named Christian Keller arrived on the footballer's equivalent of a supermarket worker's wage. A Greek nobody had heard of arrived, justified by the fact that they are Champions of Europe. Several young players returned after 'making their bones' in the provinces and little else occurred. Arrigoni would work pretty much with the promotion team and these minor retouches until the club was given the green light to proceed.

The Italian pre-season does not usually disappear into insignificance. Newspapers love reporting on transfer gossip, giving tactical analysis on the new line-ups, reporting on how long it will take Inter to be excluded from the title race. Every detail of every club's preparation is examined, from the number of weights players lift to how many kilos of pasta they consume. The summer of 2005 was rather different.

Whilst Arrigoni and the team trained and played in the background, July was a month not concentrated on football, the transfer market or tactics, but banks, complicated judicial procedures and court cases. Cimminelli, whose initial guarantee, with the 'collaboration' of Gallo had been declared a fraud, and subject to a raid at the club's office, hoped in a second appeal to the FIGC[11], based on being able to agree a deal for the spread of some of the fiscal fees over a given time - rather like Lazio had done the year earlier in spreading their enormous Scudetto[12]-winning debts over 23 years - whilst trying to locate the guarantee which would become paramount to the club's future. Without it, there would probably be no entry into Serie A.

For the appeal against the FIGC's initial decisions, Cimminelli counted on five issues. One, he had managed to agree to spread some of the

---

[11] The FIGC, is the Italian Football Federation (Federazione Italiana Giuoco Calcio and is the governing body for the game in Italy, responsible for the national team, the referees and the lower divisions. Rather perversely, the Lega Calcio (Football League) governs Serie A and Serie B as a sort of separate governing body. However, the FIGC has the greater authority.
[12] Lazio won the league championship in 2000 under Sven-Goran Eriksson having invested millions of euro on the team.

fiscal fees over a given time, settling in part some of the club's debt. Two, playing the 'injustice' card because teams like Lazio and Roma had been allowed to play in the top division despite higher debts. (However, these appeals would probably carry more weight with a non-sporting tribunals court, not the organisation responsible for those decisions). Three, acquiring a loan either from Sky - i.e. a three-year television deal paid in advance, or from a local bank to cover the guarantee. Four, that the loan he agreed with Gallo was in good faith and that he was the victim of fraud. Five, that with Torino, the club which gave Italian football its greatest ever team about to celebrate its 100th birthday, the FIGC couldn't kill the club.

Cimminelli was not to have a lot of success. The fact that he hadn't paid fiscal fees for almost five years did not gain him much respect despite the agreement to spread the payments. Two, the FIGC clearly maintained that the rules had changed in light of the previous year, and a zero tolerance policy was being adopted both on level of debt and on teams meeting application deadlines. Three, Sky were more than willing to agree a three-year tv deal with the club but not to anticipate the money. Four, Cimminelli was responsible for dealing with Gallo, and assessing with which broker he agreed the loan. Five, sentiment counts for nothing in football. The bank issue, meanwhile, would stay alive for the entire month but few people seemed prepared to back Cimminelli or trust him, probably aware that they may not see the money again.

Like over 20 other teams, mainly from the lower divisions, Torino were rebuffed by the FIGC following the second appeal. The finances were not in place to play in Serie A and the deadline had not been respected. The club, according to the highest footballing authority, was not fit to continue as a business.

The road had been blocked but hope and false promises not diminished. A month of debating and appealing would be ahead. In Italy, there is always a higher authority to appeal to. In most European countries, the FA's decision would have been final, in Italy it is merely treated as an obstacle. Cimminelli and Romero believed they were higher than justice.

The next appeal channel would be the agencies which control the finances of various businesses, the Covisoc and the Coavisoc[13]. Nobody, particularly cared or knew who they were or what they did, just that they admitted Torino into Serie A. Should their decision be negative, the next verdict would be of the sports council, CONI, then the tribunals court the Tar of Lazio[14] (the most likely commission to favour Cimminelli), which only two years earlier overturned the famous Catania case which led to the unnecessary expansion of Serie A and B. After the Tar, came the potential final appeal to the Comitato di Stato, the state council, but quite frankly should it get to that stage then it would be too late.

Cimminelli and his lawyers worked hard throughout July, although the patron was not willing to use any personal money or his company, Ergom, as a guarantee for the future of Torino Calcio. If only they'd worked a little harder earlier, who knows what the situation would have been like. But it perhaps would have only put off the inevitable. The club's debts, without the aid of a Russian billionaire, would be difficult to wipe and continue to mount. Despite famously offering the club for one euro, it seemed Cimminelli had never really tried hard to sell it. And if he had, it was no surprise that nobody had bought it considering the extend of the cancer within he club. Whatever the truth, the situation probably could have only been postponed for another year.

The feeling that Cimminelli wanted to be at the helm of the club in the prestigious year of 2006 was all too clear. However, the cost of 2006 had taken its toll on Cimminelli. He claimed that the additional 'hidden' costs of constructing the Stadio Comunale had crippled the budget and lay at the forefront of this sudden hole.

The Comunale had been left to rot, rather like the Filadelfia, following its closure in 1990. It was a stadium which even in the 1980s was well passed its sell-by date, but it was an arena which had witnessed from both of the city's teams some epic matches in Italy and Europe, international football and had always been full. The city's other team had used it as a training base for much of the 1990s but the plan to resurrect the stadium coincided with Torino's desire and necessity to move back into the city.

---

[13] The Covisoc is the agency which assess the finances of Italy's football teams. The Coavisoc is its appeals commission.
[14] The Tar of Lazio is an independent appeals commission.

However, Cimminelli was probably aware that due to the pressing need to finish building the stadium for the Winter Olympics, that the city council would have completed the cost of the project. Therefore it was a rather feeble excuse and only created an unnecessary and misguided anti-Olympic sentiment amongst Toro fans. More paramount was Cimminelli's complete mishandling of the club, dragging it continually backwards and never searching potential money making avenues nor striving to earn the respect of the club's supporters. Had he negotiated with the banks and obtained a loan or a guarantee six months earlier (seeing as the June 30 deadline to apply for the following season is always the same), he may have been able to turn the tide.

Cimminelli's arrogance, paranoia and insanity grew to new levels. 'I'll save the club if it's the last thing I do,' he barked, isolating his few allies and retreating to his bunker. He seemed like Adolf Hitler in the days before he committed suicide. 'After all the money I've invested, I'm not going to see the club die,' vowed a man who had created enemies in all circles. No Torino stalwart was willing to support him. He had shown scant regard for the FIGC deadline and created enemies in those parts, few banks or local institutions seemed willing to cover his loan, partially or totally. The hours spent combating against previous decisions made by the FIGC were counterproductive. The whole battle was a lie and Cimminelli and Romero should have surrendered earlier.

The fans naturally mobilised. These were dark times, with the future existence of the club under mass doubt. The Filadelfia on Saturday mornings, became the meeting point and a chance for tifosi to unite and make their voice heard. The promotional campaign launched by the fans called 'cercasi un presidente - we're looking for a new President' was launched in some of the newspapers, and the city's streets were soon to become battlegrounds.

On successive Saturdays the fans marched passively but with the intent of making their voice heard. On both occasions, the marches started at the Filadelfia and moved into the city. One of the gatherings was outside Chiamparino's office where cries against the mayor, Cimminelli and Romero were voiced. The mayor was targeted due to his association with the Olympics and for a perceived lack of drive in saving the club. Another misguided protest. The marches took place whilst middle age Piedmontese women poked in an out of boutiques and groups of tamarri[15] in tight yeans, Lonsdale gear and fluorescent belts, passed their usual Saturday afternoons, sitting on crash barriers and behaving like morons.

Whereas the first protest had been outside the Stadio Comunale, the second made its voice heard in the city. A couple of thousand fans marched in line making threats against the city should the team not feature in Serie A. By now, it was useless to protest against Cimminelli. The damage had been done and he was powerless to rescue the situation. He was a man on death row. The target became the city and the fans were desperate, in need of an ally, and considered anyone an enemy. In order to threaten the city, pledges and threats were voiced against the forthcoming Winter Olympics, an event Torino was stuttering to host, what represented its greatest opportunity to finally present itself as an international city and shrug of its FIAT overalls.

From winning the Host City contract in June 1999, Torino, the city, had a strange relationship with the Olympics. A climate of minimal pride, maximum suspicion. Short-sightedness particularly on behalf of the locals was palpable, with those who didn't get jobs working with the Games, unable to fathom the immediate knock-on benefits for the local economy and indeed the city.

Turin itself was almost like a Piedmontese housewife, reluctantly venturing outside the house to buy milk, without labelled clothes and full makeup. Opening itself to the world seemed to make the city even more reserved. *'Torino non si ferma mai - 'Torino always on the move'* was one of the slogans launched by the council as the city strived to find energy and momentum for the Games. A couple of impressive new venues were built in the city, the Stadio Comunale redesigned and put to use, whole areas regenerated, industrial parks created, new university sites built, historical buildings restored, environmental projects launched, an underground constructed and eventual improvements in the transport structure. Yet the Torinese would have preferred to stay behind their industrial curtain.

Torino is not a city which sells itself, nor does it want to, despite lackadaisical efforts to drive the city's potential. Its historical centre is attractive and can offer just about as much as any other Italian city from

---

[15] A tamarro is the Italian equivalent of a 'townie'

the royal square, Piazza Castello, to the designer shopping Mecca that is via Roma.

Its two main northern rivals, the livelier but greyer Milan and the depressing port city of Genoa, should enhance Turin's beauty yet Torino chooses to hide sheepishly under the Alps and promote only its grey skies, cold temperatures and misty winters. Torino's green hills should be compared to Beverly Hills, but lie shyly behind the imposing church the Grande Madre da Dio, a famous scene stealer in the *Italian Job*. Its impressive Baroque architecture seldom praised. And then there is the beautiful yet tragic Basilica of Superga, the eye which watches over the city.

The Quadrilateral area of town, offers fine bars and ethnic restaurants, but is stumbled upon and the city's best places are found, almost unwittingly, by chance. Its famous bars are perhaps too pretentious for their own good and the imperious Mole Antonellina with its spacious cinema museum is one of Europe's most underrated landmarks. The city's proximity to vineyards such as Dolcetto and Barolo, agriturisimo and slow food weekends, chocolate, cheese and gastronomic diversity should give it greater standing. Turin's proximity to the mountains make it not only accessible for winter sport weekends, but provide a stunning panorama on a clear day.

However, Turin's standing is still an industrial player. The success or failure of FIAT still dominates the city's economy and although much of FIAT's production is consigned to Eastern Europe, the car giant is still the principal representation of the city. Turin is better at promoting its faults than its beauty. The suburbs sprawl out for miles without distinction from each other, and are grey and ugly. The airport for a city hosting an international event, small and deprived of resources. The city is stiflingly hot and empty in the summer, cold, misty, foggy, grey and crowded in the winter.

In July, when the fans were marching, Turin was an open construction site. The work to construct the underground had dug up a principal artery of the city and ploughed into the suburbs. The front of the train station, a gateway to the city, not only cladden with beggars but faces a major building site. The city's two most beautiful piazzas - the enormous Piazza Vittorio Veneto, one the largest in Europe, never looked uglier -

dug up to accommodate underground parking. Piazza San Carlo, the usual epicentre for party celebrations, practically didn't exist.

Consequently, reminders of the city's construction, modernisation and spending were the backdrop to the protests. Torino fans planned a boycott of the Olympics in order to push the city into saving an institution which had a greater standing and legacy. The money spent on the Games was viewed as a waste and the debts mounted for the reconstruction of the Comunale, an excuse overplayed by Cimminelli, hardly helped.

However, with or without the Olympics, the problem still would have been the same, Cimminelli probably would have been at the helm, the debts still would have been enormous. It could be argued that for Toro, the Olympics would be a positive influence, occurring as they were in the club's centenary year. Chiamparino and the city could not afford to see a major sporting institution collapse whilst the city was about to host a prestigious international event. The embarrassment could have ruined his career and curtailed any enthusiasm for the Games. A club which had given so much to Italian football couldn't die like this.

'Senza La Serie A, gli olimpiadi non si fa - Without Serie A, the Olympics will not happen' was one of the cries along with *'senza la serie A, brucia la città - without Serie A, the city burns'*. Graffiti was a depressing addition against banks, the Olympic countdown clock in Piazza Castello, the offices of Cimminelli, the house of Romero and generally throughout the city. Ranging from *'Cimminelli, Torino non ti vuole - Cimminelli, Turin does not want you', 'Cimminelli vattene - Cimminelli go away' 'Romero muore - Romero die' 'Romero assassino di Meroni, ti togliamo i coglioni- Romero, killer of Meroni, we will cut your balls'*

The two city marches helped unite the fans, who had followed a summer of discontent through the newspapers and internet, and create a voice. The press glorified the minor acts of violence and the numbers of the ultras present (where acts violence had stretched to two bins catching fire). The marching didn't though push someone into financially back Cimminelli. And by, now, that probably was not the point. It would serve more to identify to potential saviours of the club. To prove that Torino were still alive.

The most symbolic march was the candlelight procession to Superga on a dry July evening. Around 8,000 fans made the climb from the foot of the hill at Sassi to the Basilica, in a scene of epic proportions. Again children with bicycles, old people who usually couldn't make it to the tobacconist without getting in a car, young lads with heavy flags, all carrying a lighted candle, almost making a final appeal to the heroes of Superga to save the situation. The month was like waiting for a funeral, for the life support machine to be switched off. Superga, the home of the Angels of Superga was this time home of the last prayer.

La Basilica di Superga, a structure of understated beauty, held a key strategic position having been built as a tribute to the Madonna for saving the Piedmontese army against the French over 200 years earlier. Its viewpoint over the city (when clear) is unrivalled. It's a place where young lovers who can't afford hotels rumble in cars, where live music can be enjoyed in the summer, where some of the tackiest Il Grande Torino memorabilia is sold by market traders in the car park, where the elegant museum to the side is held, where the royal tombs of the Savoy family are kept, where deep in the hills of the city, lie some off its best restaurants and worst nightclubs.

In 1976, over 200,000 people made the trip to celebrate the Scudetto, where everyday people from around the world visit the monument to the side, where every May 4th the current team (expect the year when Cimminelli's team was told not to come), officials and supporters gather for a service and tribute to the side. Sick of Cimminelli and his apathy and attitude to the club's supporters, an alternative arrangement and a very successful one was arrange in the spring of 2005. A double-header day of remembrance was organised, first mass and service at Superga followed by a match between the ultras and select Torino teams of the past at the Filadelfia.

For a month, thanks to the offerings of supporters, and sheer extraordinary volunteer work, the Filadelfia pitch was brought back to life for a football match. The Stadio Filadelfia is located in a dense residential area, on three sides of the stadium lie high-rise flats and on that evening most balconies were occupied by people who had seen any semblance of football their for nearly fifteen years, when the team last trained there.

A day of beauty and nostalgia with over 8,000 people crammed into the old ground, which apart from a few corners of the old stand and the entrance gate is, and at least to look, at no more than a park pitch. The uneven, bobbly, uncared for surface was tendered to, grass cut and pitch evened. Flags and banners decorated the sections of stands which are left, and even in their tragic and neglected state are still pillars of nostalgia. The ultras stewarded the fans behind a temporary banner as we all watched various an ultras XI play against heroes of yesteryear.

Old heroes turned out in force. Graziani did a tour of the pitch, Castellini saved a penalty, Pulici still possessed some neat touches, Sala hugged the flank. An oversized Lentini played for the younger generation team spearheaded by Silenzi, a beast of a man, unfortunately remembered for a more than tame parenthesis at Nottingham Forest. For an evening, the Filadelfia was reborn, another sign that the only way Torino could find some semblance of respect, tradition and positivity was by the efforts of the supporters. A month later, the first team made a visit to the Filadelfia, touching down on the turf for an hour to so to meet supporters and gain that extra motivational push to gain promotion. Maybe it even worked.

Throughout 2005, Torino fans aware that in the club's 99th year, it was imperative to make the centenary year as successful and positive as ever, launched campaign after campaign, trying to rebuild some of the club's old haunts (after all none of the recent Presidents had tried) and the events of July and August would reunite them even more significantly. "Whilst some organs of the media are giving us as good as dead" reported www.toronews.net, "we are clinging to the desire, like all Torino supporters, not to give up."

But Cimminelli's Torino did seem as good as dead. Following the rejection of the Covisoc and then the Coavisoc, the appeals commission, the situation worsened and time was running out as the Cimminelli and Romero prepared for the appeal to CONI, the last level of sporting justice. Every rejection met with another protest the cries of "Se il Toro se ne va, bruceremo la città - If Toro disappear, we will burn the city," which became the city's anthem in July 2005.

The Turin-based San Paolo bank was seen as one of the potential saviours. On the 8th July they were even said to have been ready to pay the loan. San Paolo was a major sponsor of the Winter Olympics and it was believed that it could act as a guarantee for preserving one of the city's sporting institutions. San Paolo, though, were not prepared to cover all of Cimminelli's misgivings, agreeing only to cover a small section of the debt, and despite threats from some of the more vociferous supporters about a boycott of the bank, San Paolo never offered any additional aid. Indeed, in a situation so desperate and seeing as the new Stadio Comunale was a Torino possession, it remained surprising that no major long-term sponsorship deal with the stadium was agreed. Cimminelli again maintained; "We're expecting one thing- that we'll play in Serie A. And I'm 100% certain we will do it."

Another bank, Unicredit, seemed more willing to cover a great part of the loan, but not significantly enough too eventually help Cimminelli out. The Calabrese was in a desperate corner. Months earlier he had offered the club for a euro, now for nothing, but with debts of 51 million euros and a stadium to finish constructing, who would want it?

One evening it appeared Cimminelli had found a saviour, when a loan was agreed only for the unnamed party to mysteriously have a change of heart the morning after. Urban rumours surfaced about who could have been behind that change of heart. In the meantime any potential interested parties were remaining just that from entrepreneurs Danilo Coppola to Luigi Zunino. Only Sergio Rodda and a small consortium had moved forward to sanction a potential Lodo Petrucci.

What was worrying about the appeals was the scarce amount of time the Torino hearing received. Of all the teams in dire straights, Torino certainly the most dire. Messina's problem was related to a single tax problem which didn't seem unresovable and they were eventually reprieved by the Tar of Lazio. For Cimminelli, there was no hiding. The CONI rejected Torino's appeal without caution, prompting another idiotic statement from Romero: "It was the best kind of rejection we could hope for."

By the time of the appeal at the Tar of Lazio, Torino fans had grown sick of tribunals and desperate legal attempts at saving a club which by now was all but dead. And so were the chances of playing in Serie A. In Messina the supporters blocked the ferries entering the city, in Genoa the railtracks and motorways were sabotaged. Torino fans did not see the situation as an legal injustice (despite the Lazio precedence), by now it was a chance to be rid of Cimminelli, who after the rejection by the Tar, still searched for a last-minute attempt to salvage the club and remained convinced he could. He always claimed that the appeal would be long, but like the promotion go successfully to the wire. The night before the Comitato di Stato made the final verdict on he club, he claimed to have 'one of my men abroad finding a solution which would go into the night.' Turin waited but hardly with baited breath whilst Cimminelli tried to find the guarantee of at least 18 million euros which would guarantee Serie A football. This in the knowledge that no team had ever gone bankrupt after gaining promotion. Another record awaited this mysterious club and disastrous owner.

Chapter 5 - Torino Calcio RIP

Whoever Cimminelli's man was or wherever he went we will never know. But he didn't come back with a cheque or a loan and within hours, Cimminelli was relieved of his duties as owner of Torino Calcio.

The Comitato di Stato predictably upheld the verdicts of the previous tribunals, declaring Torino Calcio not fit to continue business. The FA confirmed that Cimmi and Tilli's Torino didn't exist any more. For precision the decision was sanctioned at 18:10 on the 9th August. Torino Calcio still had not been declared bankrupt but no longer ceased to exist as a football club. Cimminelli was still free to continue fight against bankruptcy in the coming months, with a likely tribunal hearing in November.

Perugia and Salernitana were also to have that same fate making the previous Serie B's campaign almost worthless. With champions Genoa eventually demoted to Serie C1 for a match-fixing scandal, the second promotion place was reopened. Under the rules of the previous season had the team finishing third, which with Torino theoretically taking Genoa's second place was Perugia, finishing ten points ahead of fourth placed Treviso, then the first three would go up and the playoff system rendered unnecessary. Perugia duly finished ten points ahead of Treviso. Therefore because of Genoa's indiscretion, and had it been brought to light earlier, the long month of June and the playoffs, were worth nothing. Torino and Perugia like Empoli would have gone straight into Serie A (and sent straight back down again).

In the end it would have made little difference, but maybe without the distraction of the playoffs, the respective clubs may have had more time to get their finances in order or at least submit the necessary paperwork on time. The playoff was declared void a second time when seeing as Torino were botched from Serie A, the team deserving of their place -

Perugia - were also declared bankrupt. Therefore, the two teams who finished fifth and six, Treviso and Ascoli and defeated in the playoff semi-finals were promoted to Serie A by default.

Ascoli were hardly a team who set Serie B alight and had already sold their two top goalscorers whilst preparing for their rightful Serie B campaign. However, they were a club who had tasted the top-flight before. Treviso, in the meantime, were Serie A debutants without a stadium fit for the top-flight, although a city with a rich sporting traditions, housing the national champions of basketball, volleyball and rugby.

Of rich irony, Treviso had appointed Ezio Rossi as coach in the summer – the man sacked by Torino with two games of the regular 2004-05 season remaining. With promotion seemingly at the door, he led his team to two insipid away draws at an already relegated Catanzaro and then at Ternana and paid the price for his pathetic motivational skills and inability to change the course of a game. Rossi was replaced by Zaccarelli who took the team by the balls and led them to promotion.

Rossi claimed that 'the promotion was 90% his' which on the basis that he led the team for 90% of the season was true. However, few believe that without his 'sudden' sacking, that the team would have been promoted. Rossi, a player raised at the Stadio Filadelfia, a fearsome central defence who played with character and heart and sports a rugby player's facial defects, was a surprisingly placid Coach, and after almost two stuttering seasons at the club was fired shortly before his contract was to expire anyway.

After his first season, the 2003-04 campaign, Rossi was given a reprieve, something rare in Italian football circles, mainly because Cimminelli couldn't afford to sack him. During his second season he spent most of it like a man of death row, and rarely had the confidence of the club's supporters. Rossi famously had two expressions – one with a baseball hat, the other without.

Due to the demise of Torino, Genoa and Perugia, Pescara, Catanzaro and Vicenza were reinstated into Serie B having been relegated to Serie C1. Therefore from last year's second division only Empoli had been promoted on right. Of the relegated teams, only Venezia had gone (but due to their bankruptcy), joined by Perugia (bankrupt), Salernitana (bankrupt) and Genoa (match fixing). Therefore, last year's Serie B table may as well have been designed by bank statements and judicial proceedings.

It was a situation which made a further mockery of Italian football. Albeit, this new hard line approach to finances and match fixing, should be commended, it needs to be applied year in and year out. Serie A used to be one of the most organised, professional leagues in Europe. However, in the last decade something has been left to rot. From racism to violence, match fixing to fake passports, financial problems to failed drug tests, poor results in Europe and at the World Cup to television problems, depleted stadiums to spitting players to objects launched from the terraces on the pitch. Once a league rigidly organised with eighteen teams in the top-flight, 34 rounds of fixtures, Sunday afternoon kick-offs bar one evening game, Serie A has struggled to come to terms with the modernisation of football and the fragmented power groups in charge of the game.

The economic crisis and overspending of the early 1990s has caused the near death of some of the great piazzas. It's hardly a great spectacle to see cities like Napoli, Torino, Bologna and Genoa in the lower divisions, Fiorentina likewise until recently. Due to an appeal made by a tribunals court by Catania regarding Siena's use of the squalified player (he in question, Luigi Martinelli, would become a future Torino player) in a youth team match, Serie B was unnecessarily expanded and consequently so was Serie A. Whilst the rest of Europe downsized, Serie A increased but the quality hasn't. Romance has a home in football, but Serie A has never been so abounded with teams from small towns like Empoli, Siena, Chievo, Lecce, Reggina, Ascoli, Treviso, Messina and Livorno.

The television money has only served to make the top three even richer and it's reached a stage where a surprise package like Verona in 1985 doesn't win the title but barely qualifies for Europe. Not that football in other major countries is significantly more democratic, but seeing anyone break the stranglehold of the three top club (not that Inter have much of a say on the field of play) is difficult. Roma and Lazio managed it for a year each but risked sheer bankruptcy in the intervening years.

The problems of the summer of 2005 forced the fixture list to be produced only two weeks before the season started, most clubs didn't have a television deal and fought over the crumbs on offer, seven to eight teams didn't know which league they were going to take part in and the change in kick-off times, especially in Serie B, only served to antagonise supporters.

Having so many appeals courts and tribunals makes the process lengthy, confusing and open to corruption. Having two footballing bodies like the Lega Calcio and the Federcalcio likewise causes problems and the Lega Calcio is also presided by the man who is also vice-President of one of the country's biggest clubs - Milan's Adriano Galliani. Not something which rests easily in a country where suspicion reigns.

The Federcalcio have promised that from the summer of 2006 to put an end to the non-sporting appeals tribunals and also the system of 'reinstating' relegated teams by virtue of their previous league position. Teams, if necessary, will be 'reinstated' on 'sporting merit', which seems to open the door for further corruption and problems, ie. giving precedent to great teams in difficulty.

Italian football is still unable to exploit certain financial possibilities. The domestic cup competition remains something relegated to inconvenient slots in the calendar and is almost a consolation prize. Awarding Champions' League qualification possible via the cup competition could be one avenue, coupled with making the Coppa Italia a knockout competition drawn randomly in the English format and giving it a weekend slot at least for a few rounds, together with one-off final on neutral territory.

Merchandise and marketing is exploited by few teams, video surveillance and policing in stadiums minimal, organised away travel at the hands of fans rather than clubs. Too much suspicion surrounds the game and too much emphasis placed on the performance of the referee. Italian television stations spend all week commenting on refereeing performances, and re-running refereeing mistakes. Nowhere in the world is the more attention paid as to who is refereeing the weekend's fixtures.

Not that Toro supporters were too bothered about referees on the 9th August 2005. When the news broke at the club's training base in Acqui Terme, tears were had and if anything the players had been kept in the dark about the situation. Zaccarelli had done his best to calm the atmosphere, Cimminelli and Romero had even made a brief visit to Macugnaga in July to confirm that the situation would have a positive end. The players believed them. Even a couple of days before the club folded they were still anaemically active in the slow transfer market, presenting the Honduran international Edgar Alvarez to the press in a perhaps pale bid to convince themselves that the situation could still have a positive end.

More telling had been the story of 'keeper Luca Castellazzi who was signed from Brescia. His stay at the club lasted a few days before he decided, perhaps wisely, that the situation was too insecure and promptly moved to Sampdoria. The players had believed and wanted to believe the words of President Romero. He, however, was the most hated figure on the day the news broke out.

"He took us for a ride," blasted Maniero, one of the more vocal protestors. "What that man does, and what he says is all a lie." Coach Daniele Arrigoni already confirmed his departure: "I came here knowing the situation," he admitted, "And am proud to have been Coach of Torino even if just for a month. I want to come back and honour this club." Gianluca Comotto who had been captain for a mere few friendlies admitted: "It's like having a hole in my heart that I couldn't have led this club in Serie A as we deserved on the field of play." "It's a sensation of emptiness and despair," said Mantovani.

Their summer had not been entirely useless. Whatever their destiny, the players needed to keep fit and be in form for whoever they played for. Their season and futures were guaranteed. The atmosphere was depressing as the team had built a close unity. However, for most their lives would go on, and some had already archived the experience.

The players agreed to honour the friendly which would take place the day after and say goodbye to the supporters. A friendly against Acqui Terme in a small stadium near Lago Maggiore was played under surreal circumstances in front of supporters who pleaded for players to stay and thanked them for their efforts. '99 anni di storia finiti in vergonga - 99 years of history finished in embarrassment,' read a large banner. The friendly helped recapture some of the feelings which must have been felt by the young players who took to the field in the first match after Superga. During the cries against Cimminelli, some of the players, including Maniero even joined in. For the record the goals scored were by Robert Acquafresca, a brace from Keller and strikes from Liborio Bongiovanni and Quagliarella.

Whilst Cimminelli had tried to rescue the club from his mess, Torino had already applied for the Lodo Petrucci and thanks to Chiamparino, the consortium led by Rodda and the water group Smat, were already registered albeit temporarily for a new campaign in Serie B. However, these were crumbs of consolation on such a grey day.

For the supporters, admittedly a weight was removed, not only the riddance of Cimminelli and Romero but a summer of confusion, angst, depression and false hope. Not that the situation was any clearer, nor the future any rosier. The fans had watched the team play across the country, gain a dramatic and hard-fought promotion, only for the prize to be Serie B football, a summer of suffering and the death of the old club.

The new club was a more attractive proposition, rid of those debts, but there was still no guarantee that the money the club desperately needed to revive Toro's past and steer it to a brighter future was going to appear.

The Stadio Filadelfia reborn for a day. May 4th 2005 (P Bourne)

Torino supporters take to the streets in protest against Cimminelli and Romero. July 2005 (P Bourne)

The Torino mascot sits lonely and abandoned under a tribune at the Stadio Filadelfia. August 2005 (P Bourne)

A message left outside Romero's residence. (P Bourne)

Patience running thin outside the Municipio. August 2005. (P Bourne)

Peter Bourne at the main Turin Central Cemetery next to the tribute built to Il Grande Torino. November 2005 (T Caso)

Torino President Urbano Cairo parades the Olympic Torch at Superga on the eve of the XX Olympic Winter Games (Granatissimo)

The imperious and formidable Il Grande Torino (Granatissimo)

Torino Football Club 2005-06 (Granatissimo)

Turin and the River Po looking spectacular during the Winter Olympics. February 2006. (P Bourne)

Chapter 6 - Traitors?

The few days following August 9th were strange to say the least. Torino Calcio no longer existed and Torino Football Club were not yet born. The new club had no assets, no debts, no players, no stadium, no employees, no Coach, no teambus, no club headquarters, no club shop, no sponsorship, no merchandise, no logo, no nothing.

Ninety-nine years of history couldn't be distinguished because of the negligence of one man and double standards of others and because of over a million supporters prepared to fight for a new, clean beginning without forgetting the unique foundations and story of the old club. The new club would carry a new name and have a new start but still carry the same weight of history and expectation.

The transfer rumours heard during the Cimminelli-cheque-or-no-cheque-saga during July regarding players already signing pre-contracts with new clubs proved true. 'Keeper Stefano Sorrentino had already left for Greek side AEK Athens of all destinations before most of the trouble had exploded. And they paid a fee for him too. Luca Mezzano, my neighbour, and captain Diego De Ascentis were both out of contract and had seemed certain to leave anyway. The club had offered them nothing after six months of negotiations. The former received little communication regarding a renewal and eventually joined Bologna, the latter unable to agree terms having signed an extortionate contract during the early Cimminelli months after signing for almost five million euros from Milan. De Ascentis joined Genoa but following the fall of that club moved onto Livorno. A number of other players had already left the promotion team even before the troubles began. The three players loaned from Chievo - Sasa Bruno, Carbone and Emanuele Pesaresi - had all already returned to base. Codrea went back to Palermo, Gianluca Berti to Empoli.

Unfortunately, the voices surrounding some of the younger players already sold off to Serie A sides were also true. And on the 9th August when they were liberated from their former contracts, began the scramble to sign up the Torino talent. Fabio Quagliarella, a striker of potential, an eye for goal and club youth product was quick to move onto pastures new. He was the sort of player the club for whom the new club could have begun to mould a future out of. A player who had received a lot of support from the club following some difficult moments in the promotion campaign. Quagliarella eventually joined Ascoli via Udinese and will probably enjoy a glittering career.

Also on his way to Ascoli was Comotto, elected captain during the summer, but a player unloved by the Toro fans despite his determination on the field. A player of limited technical ability Comotto is also a known supporter of team of the team from the other side of the city. Comotto's parting shot at the Lodo Petrucci group, hinting that they were incompetent, didn't smooth his departure. He initially joined Roma, who signed him more as a trade asset, and promptly loaned him to the Marchè club.

Another bright young prospect Giovanni Marchese, fresh from a year-long loan at Treviso and U-21 international recognition, moved to Chievo where he would join other ex-Toro youth products in Sergio Pellissier, Franco Semioli and Simone Tiribocchi. Galling for Torino to lose such players to a team hailing effectively from a suburb of Verona (mainly due to Cimminelli and Mazzola, and their lack of faith in the club's youth team).

Lanky defender Peccarisi slipped off in tears rather surprisingly to Triestina. Peccarisi was one of the few players who would have given his right leg to play for the new club but the Lodo Petrucci group never returned his phone calls. The popular but not indispensable Conticchio moved to Cagliari and two players signed during the summer - the Greek Alexis Nastorous and Dane Christopher Keller were snapped like hungry hounds by Chievo and Lazio respectively.

Indeed Lazio, the club of huge debts who had survived extinction a year earlier, were amongst the most hungry for Toro blood. As well as Keller, they signed Mudingayi, a player who Toro launched from nowhere and showed scant regard for sentiment. However, it was clear that the modern footballer looks after No 1, the players autonomous from their agents few and far between, players who identify themselves to a public, a shirt, a story rather than a paycheck, players with the minimum regard or respect for the tifoseria, barely exist. Lucarelli, again, one of few.

"Nobody asked me to stay," blasted Mudingayi, "My heart is still in Turin and I feel let down by the way it finished and the way Cimminelli made us believe survival was possible until the last minute." Most players reiterated that the Lodo Petrucci group didn't move quick enough to secure their services for the new club. Perhaps the players moved too quickly to avoid making that decision.

Pinga, another player for whom Toro had a built a future and nurtured when things didn't go well, also left. His destination of Treviso seemed both modest and untactful. Treviso, the team to benefit from Toro's demise could offer Serie A football, but a sparse profile, public and chances of remaining in the top-flight. Pinga's introverse, atypically Brazilian character probably suits the small town atmosphere where pressure is non-existent. Appealing for Pinga was a reunion with Rossi, the man who had he not been sacked by Toro in May would have dragged the club into Serie C, having seen this summer's demotion. Pinga's sublime talent deserved a better destination. Torino fans would have swallowed the pill more easily.

Two players who seemed destined to stay at Torino for life and who - aside from the odd loan spell in the provinces - had been there for life were Mantovani and Balzaretti. Clean faced, good boys, who identified themselves with the supporters and were always the first to kiss the badge under the curva at the end of the game. Both claimed to cry when the club went bust. Both had made declarations of eternal love for the club. Both were loved like children by the tifosi. Both were to leave.

Mantovani was first. He didn't even hang around for the club's funeral before landing himself a new, lucrative contract. He was to finish at the primary school for members of Torino's nursery - Chievo. However it was apparent that he had signed for another club before being parked at Chievo. That 'other club' initially seemed to be Inter before being revealed as the co-tenants of the Stadio Delle Alpi. Mantovani crossed where he shouldn't have crossed, had cut his ties and place in Torino's history. And sacrificed his dignity. Men like this aren't worthy of the Granata shirt. "It was an inevitable ending," claimed Mantovani. "Cimminelli and Romero took us and the fans for a ride making us belief everything would finish with a happy ending. I had offers from important clubs and in life the train doesn't always pass twice." At 21 years old and an U-21 international regular, however, you think it would.

Whilst Mantovani hid in Verona, Balzaretti took more time in deciding his future. More than Mantovani, he was the symbol of Toro. A player who never complained to referees, never gave in, never dived, never made an out of place tackle, never a piece of controversy. A player typified by his reaction to an opposition goal in a Torino versus Catania game when he congratulated his ex-colleague Ferrante after he put the Sicilians ahead.

Balzaretti gained a reputation as a promising, athletic wing-back with a lot of potential. Lazio, them again, seemed the most keen for his signature, Parma, Siena and Ascoli made tentative enquiries before Roma moved onto the horizon. "Roma is an attractive prospect, with great players and a great city," admitted Balza, 24 hours before deciding his future. Most Toro fans would have swallowed Roma, not what was to happen.

The rumour began on the internet. "**ve went Balzaretti," "Balzaretti in talks with **ve." Nobody wanted nor believed it. However, on the evening of the 15th August, I turned on the television to hear Moggi announcing the arrival of Balzaretti. I not only didn't want to believe it but physically didn't digest it and ignored it.

The following morning, *Tuttosport* ran the enormous headline "Balza alla **ve". Treacherous, shirt-kissing, false turncoat of a bastard. Balzaretti had done exactly what should have been in his DNA not to do. He had moved across the city. For Torino supporters, having lost Serie A football and having witnessed the terrible month of July, having passed an awful summer this was like the final nail in the coffin. Balzaretti and his goodness, his Torino spirit, was one of the last positive things to cling onto.

"It was a hard decision," he said rather obviously. "But I only moved to **ve because I was promised that I would stay and not be sold. I can't lie that the thought of staying in Turin, my home, was a big factor." Balza is likely to be reminded about his mistake and his decision to stay close to his mother's cooking and ironing. Fortunately for him, in the meantime and within days, Toro fans would have other figures to hate.

"You will finish in hospital," "We want you dead," ran a few of the less volatile internet messages. I took the more mundane route of destroying my Balzaretti signed photo, the only footballer autograph I own, and deciding he wasn't worth worrying about.

Balzaretti became the seventh Torino player to join **ve. The first was Riccardo Carapellese in 1952 who was followed by future coach Simoni in 1967 and then Aldo Serena in 1985, whose move across the city was amongst the most contested. Following Calleri's dismantling of the club in the summer of 1994 both captain Fusi and Croatian Robert Jarni joined the Bianconeri. The last player to make the switch being Gianluca Pessotto in 1995 who went on to serve **ve for over a decade.

The message for messrs Mudingayi, Comotto, Quagliarella and above all Mantovani and Balzaretti was clear. Torino gave you everything. You gave back little. You won't be welcome back or nostalgicised. As a reward you could have signed contracts with the new club on the promise you would go ahead and play in Serie A, but at least have made some money for a club waking from the dead. However, due to the events of the following weeks, Balzaretti's treachery was briefly forgotten.

One notice of loyalty came from former coach Mondonico, the man who led Torino to their last major trophy and who offered to work for the new club for free.

Chapter 7 - The men who saved the club: The Lodisti

The new Torino Football Club, as it would be called, began to emerge from the ashes of Torino Calcio. There were few guarantees left for supporters to cling on to. The tifosi relieved that the disastrous Cimminelli era had ended now hoped the future didn't spawn an owner quite so incompetent and disrespectful to the club's traditions.

The reality that the promotion had been fruitless, that the heroes of last year had gone, that Balzaretti now wore black and white stripes, that the club were back in Serie B and during the entire summer no significant entrepreneur had come forward to take control, was sinking in. It was time for a deep breath before assessing the situation, rather like a ravaged country liberated after a long, bloody war.

Torino had been rescued from the threat of fourth division thanks to the intervention of a number of people. Chiamparino had fought to find investment to guarantee the eight million euros needed to enable the club to take part in Serie B, a guarantee promised by the water company Smat. Smat may never have to pay the fee in the event that a bidder came forward before the new club was recognised as a company, which was a matter of weeks away.

The other heroes in the rescue of the club were the group of men to become known as the 'Lodisiti', a consortium of supporters, formed mainly of local businessman prepared to takeover the running of the club and ultimately invest in it. The central figures of this group were Sergio Rodda, an industrialist and head of the Piccoli Imprenditori Torinesi - small local entrepreneurs - a man who had been active since July in moving the Lodo Petrucci idea forward. His chief partner was the local politician and lawyer Pierluigi Marengo, who would become a major figure in the forthcoming weeks.

As Torino supporter and renowned television comic Piero Chiamberetti commented: "One thing is certain, thanks to the men of the Lodi we haven't disappeared from the history of football or from the playsation which still includes teams from Serie B." Who that playstation team would have as its heroes remained to be seen.

Eva Henger, her of the big breasts, and a Torino supporter due to her compatriot Erbstein's association with the club in the 1940s added: "I hope that this sad month for Torino supporters is behind us. Our fans deserve a place in the football that counts - in Serie A." Other famous Torino supporters like the rock group Statuto, the omnipresent long-legged television presenter Simona Ventura and even leading politicians like Nicolo Mancino were incited to promote the Torino cause.

There was much appreciation for the Lodisti but little long-term faith and the supporters still hoped for a money-magnet to move forward. One of the rumoured favourites to become President of the new club was Franco Arese, once a famous Italian athlete over the 800m distance, Torino supporter, head of the Italian Athletics Federation and owner of the Asics sportswear company, based just outside of Turin. Arese though had always distanced himself from taking over the club, offering his company's services as kit manufacturer but little else.

Others looked at rich Piedmontese industrialists who maybe hadn't come forward earlier because they were put off by Cimminelli's debts. However, appeals to men who had little interest in football didn't seem a logical step. Companies like Ferrero, the world famous chocolate producer, and Lavazza, the coffee distributor, are both Piedmontese institutions but bar the odd sponsorship deal (Ferrero's Kinder brand was once the shirt sponsor of the Torino youth team), neither were interested in investing in football.

Chiamparino appealed to Ernesto Pellegrini who had been the successful President of Inter before Moratti, but Pellegrini declined, stating: "It would be an honour to help Torino, a club with a rich tradition, but unless you are 100% convinced by a decision then there is little point in acting on other people's wishes and deluding people. I'm not sure I want to return to football."

Therefore Marengo, a man who had campaigned actively against Cimminelli regarding the misuse of the Filadelfia, and Rodda moved forward until an interest buyer became available. In the meantime, the pair were joined by a small-time investor by the name of Luca Giovannone, a businessman whose company Vita Serena imported nurses from eastern Europe. The company's feeble website said a lot about his economic potential.

Giovannone offered to finance the initial running of the club, until someone with a greater capital came forward. He admitted that he had no ambition beyond helping the club out in this difficult moment. A self professed Torino fanatic and self-made man, Giovannone hails from the same part of Italy as Graziani, hence his perverse passion for the club. His capital was limited but enough to help the Lodisiti build a team strong enough to offer a 'dignified' Serie B campaign. Rodda, Marengo and Giovannone were roundly lauded by Torino supporters.

In the event of nobody with greater capital coming forward, the plan was to adopt a Barcelona-style philosophy for the club, with supporters having large shares and a say in the running of the club. This move would be exercised within weeks when the club could be declared as a company should nobody come forward. After a summer in which, only the supporters of Toro came out with any credit, it seemed the noble and just option.

Whilst it was a future which promised greater dignity and a greater respect for Torino's past, there were no guarantees for the future of the team nor any immediate return to the upper echelons of the Italian game. There was a reality check when Paolo Stringara was named as Coach of the new club. Stringara, in his early 40s, had never coached beyond Serie C, had been without work for two years and had been sacked three times already in his short career. The highlight of his career had been a spell at Livorno sandwiched between less fruitful times at Viterbo and La Spezia in the Italian football backwater. "I just ask one thing," pleaded Stringara on his arrival at the club, "Not to be judged now or pre-judged based on what is written in the football annuals about my last few years. I want to be judged once I've begun my work."

If Stringara was something of a gamble, the choice of Director General was also a contentious appointment. Turin-born Michele Padovano was not most people's selection. Padovano is a Torino fan but at 39-years old a novice in such a position. More problematic was his past as a Bianconeri player. Despite his self-proclaimed love of Torino, something he maintained throughout his career, he never played for the Granata but enjoyed a few years under Marcello Lippi's all-conquering black and white side, before spending an unsuccessful and injury ravaged spell in England with Crystal Palace.

What's more, Padovano enjoyed a close relationship with Italian football's public enemy number one, Moggi, a man who had made no secret of his feelings that Torino were a unfortunate obstacle for the Bianconeri. Former railway station controller Moggi was once Director General of Torino before being discarded along with the rest of the club in the troubled summer of 1993. Moggi's impact on ****ntus is tremendous and influence within the Italian game is without equal. His son, Alessandro, is one of the country's most significant agents running the powerful Gea group and Padovano seemed very much part of this family.

Padovano and Stringara were the first two major appointments and they were left free to start assembling a team from scratch although without significant money to spend. Their task was to find experienced non-contract players with a hunger to prove a point, youngsters desperate to make the grade or players unwanted by their current employers.

The first signings included defender Luca Ungari, a player discarded by Modena. He was joined by former teammate and Bosnian international Vedin Music, another player confined to the Serie B wastepaper basket that summer.

A 'keeper was found in the form of Arezzo's Angelo Pagotto, once a hot prospect on Milan's books before being banned for cocaine use and since when his career had never recovered. Senegalese defender Diaw Doudou, famed for his concentration lapses, arrived from Bari. Former **ve youth product and another self-professed Toro fan Andrea Gentile signed to add creativity to the midfield.

Padovano promoted the club to potential signings by announcing the signing of former Bologna and Italy winger Carlo Nervo. However, the 34-year old, due to family problems, saw his arrival in Turin delayed and then due to the saga which was to follow never even arrived in the Piedmont capital. Padovano's biggest signing was a non-event.

Injury-prone but highly-rated midfielder Andrea Ardito signed up from Siena and young striker Claudio De Souza from Lazio. It was on paper, a very average group of players. Padovano also secured the services of five of the club's former players. The first to sign up being last season's second choice goalkeeper Alberto 'Jimmy' Fontana. Few could comment on Fontana's attributes as a footballer. In a decade long career he had barely played outside of Serie C1 and had only amassed 66 league appearances.

Turin born and bred, Fontana had joined Toro in the summer of 2003 following a mass swap of unwanted players with Palermo and Roma. In his first three years in Turin, he featured just seven times in the league without making any major mistakes nor major saves. However, his values as a person were more apparent and appreciated. He organised regular charity work on behalf of a children's hospital, inviting teammates to make regular visits and give hope to seriously ill or dying children.

Fontana is a self-professed ultrà, a man who if destiny had not put him on the Torino bench, would be in the curva. Following the promotion win over Perugia, Fontana was famously filmed climbing the crossbar before taking a dive from the top of the goal to the turf. When the team played the friendly against Acqui Terme to say goodbye to supporters, Fontana left the pitch in tears vowing his allegiance to the club even should they finished in the local amateur leagues. These were not empty words like those of his former teammates.

The Curva Maratona is referred to as the 12th man, and no Torino player can wear the 12 shirt as it was reserved for the fans. Fontana by virtue of being the second-choice 'keeper and a fan, is the real 12th man. His loyalty to the cause was rewarded with a three-year deal. A cynic would say that Fontana didn't exactly have a lot of other offers, but it's unlikely even had his situation been different he would have trod the path of Mantovani and Balzaretti.

With the arrival of the Pagotto, Fontana was again pencilled down to be the 12th player, but he approached the new project with great enthusiasm and took it upon himself to recite the history of the club to his new colleagues. The remaining players from Cimminelli's Torino to re-sign included former youth team striker Liborio Bongiovanni, who had already made an appearance for the first team and another ex-youth team player in Brazilian winger Ronaldo Vanin who had just spent a successful year on loan at Avellino.

Playmaker Carlos Marinelli, the underachieving and mercurial Argentine, returned for his third spell at the club. Marinelli, once rated as the 127th heir to Maradona, had lost his way following massive promise as a youngster that led to a million euro move from Boca Juniors to Middlesbrough. The final ex-player to sign was 19-year old midfielder Tommaso 'Ricky' Vailatti, a player of massive potential, who spurned other offers to stay with his home-town club. Vailatti was greeted positively by fans and made some harsh remarks about ex-teammate Balzaretti. "You can join ****ntus," admitted Vailatti, "but not if only a few days earlier you were expressing eternal love to Torino. It's betrayal." For most of these players, it was the chance to make something of their careers, to impress in a team and a club which although decimated to the bones still held a certain, unique and magnetic appeal.

Marengo and Rodda based the club headquarters near the Porta Nuova train station in an apartment on Corso Vittorio Emanuele II. That area of town in August, like Turin, was deserted. In the weeks when Padovano was frenetically trying to build a team, the only people you saw in that part of Turin were footballers. There was a team to build and quickly.

As Marengo commented: "We were the only people to save Torino from the coffin. We have worked hardly and honestly and will continue to do so." However, when the club met to begin its record-breakingly delayed pre-season there was still a sense of sadness. Around eight players met in a piazza which had witnessed just weeks earlier, passionate protests against Cimminelli. They arrived independently and in their own gear.

The team had no kit and the players initially trained in their own clothes. Marengo, Giovannone and Rodda still had to find the club a place to train, equipment, a hotel, club offices not to mention begin a season ticket campaign, negotiate television deals, sponsorships, reinstall the faith in the supporters, restore the club's former honours still under the ownership of Cimminelli, construct a youth system, resign a deal for the Stadio Comunale and renegotiate a contract to play at the Delle Alpi for another year. There was a lot to be done. Watching eight players begin to train in their own clothes on a bumpy pitch in Giaveno seemed a long way from constructing a team even worthy of the Playstation never mind Serie B promotion.

The Lega Calcio allowed Torino to start their season two weeks later than the other teams, on the 10th September. The first two scheduled games against Pescara and Bari would be rearranged and Toro's season would start against Albinoleffe, the only visiting team to have ever visited the Grande Torino museum at Superga. However, there was still less than a matter of weeks to fulfil the pressing requirements. As Marengo claimed: "At my first meeting at the FA, I felt like a boy during his first day at school." This quote spoke volumes about his ability to face the task ahead.

Chapter 8 - The takeover battle: Cairo v Giovannone

On Thursday 18th August, emerged a notice which Torino fans had been waiting over twenty years for - a rich and respected Piedmontese entrepreneur wanted to buy the club. His name? Urbano Cairo.

Cairo was interviewed the following day in *La Stampa* by the respected Granata fan and journalist Massimo Gramellini. His message was concise and positive. Cairo wanted to buy Torino FC, promising to invest heavily in the club whilst leading the team back to Serie A and to the upper echelons of the Italian game. In a word, the messiah the fans had been praying for had arrived.

Cairo's passion for Torino was inherited from his parents who had watched Il Grande Torino and Cairo recalled hearing stories about his mother's tears after the post-Superga team suffered a 7-1 loss at Milan in October 1949. Cairo was able to recall the 1975-76 title winning team even pronouncing Pulici correctly and not 'Pulicio' like Cimminelli. He passed the history test with top marks.

Cairo's rise to richness was rapid. He was a former assistant of Silvio Berlusconi during the early 1980s before becoming commercial director and director general of the Pubitalia '80, an administration of the Mondadori publishing group. Cairo Communications, his prospering business, was formed in 1995 and had enjoyed a decade of solid and growing success.

His career path highlighted his ambition and brilliance. In July 1981, at the age of 24, and having finished a summer studies in the United States, Cairo put his mind to work. Having read an interview with the entrepreneur Berlusconi, Cairo telephoned the future Italian Prime Minister asking him for a meeting. Cairo spoke to Berlusconi's secretary announcing that he had 'two massive ideas to discuss.' Eventually and after much pleading Cairo met with Berlusconi's no 2, Marcello Dell'Utri, who discovered in Cairo a bright and talented young man and promptly arranged an meeting with Berlusconi who was to offer Cairo the chance to become his assistant.

Cairo was finishing his obligatory national service, completing his military services in the morning and then working for Berlusconi's Fininvest in the afternoon and evenings before finding the time to complete his university thesis. He soon gained the reputation as workaholic but also a man prepared to give his time to people. He is also famously superstitious, and reportedly prefers to make major decisions, if possible, on the 19th of the month - 19 being his lucky number. His ex-colleagues at Pubitalia defined him as 'a brilliant organiser of people, an excellent salesman but with a human touch.' In the early 90s, Berlusconi made Cairo head of the Mondadori group, Cairo having excelled at Pubitalia, but the move was also political as some of Cairo's jealous peers feared his close relationship with Berlusconi. From his spell at Mondadori, Cairo built the experience and contacts which in 1995 saw him start his own business.

His company, The Cairo Communications group, controls seven sectors from television channels, to advertising spaces, to web searches to directories and in the year of 2005 alone made 200 million euros and after the giant Mondadori became the second in the Italian in the field of publishing weekly magazines (titles ranging from *For Men* to *Airone* to *Bell'italia* to *Gardenia*), and the exclusive advertising rights for the national channel La7.

Cairo entered the fray for Toro ownership late, believing the club was already in good hands and having been unsure about taking on such a challenge. He moved after the considerably poorer Giovannone emerged as the first entrepreneur to offer financial guarantees to the Lodisti, albeit only 180,000 euro. Cairo was prompted into action following a phone call from Mayor Sergio Chiamparino, whose role in the Torino affair over the coming weeks would become enormous. "I received a phone call from my lawyer Giovanni Trombetta who informed me that Chiamparino wanted to talk to me," revealed Cairo. "He said he had heard good things about me and asked me if I was interested in taking over Torino. I responded that I would need two or three days to think about it."

"On Saturday the 13th August," continued Cairo, "I went with my family on holiday to Forte of the Marmi, and instead of going to the beach slowly transformed the hotel into a branch office with football coaches and directors coming and going." Cairo began to examine what was behind running a football club, examining every detail of the business, before making an offer for the club.

Chiamparino sponsored Cairo's offer, having understandable doubts as to how far the Lodisti could take the club alone: "I have faith in Cairo's offer. It seems similar to the Fiorentina case a few years ago when the Dalla Valle family took over following bankruptcy. Cairo has a strong, positive offer. It's a serious thing. People like him emerge just once every 20 years."

Cairo already announced that former Modena and Brescia Coach, Gigi De Biasi, 'a tipo tosto - a lively sort,' would be the new Coach. De Biasi admitted to researching who Cairo was on the internet before interrupting his holiday in Austria to meet Cairo in the Forte of the Marmi. Cairo was wise in avoiding heavy promises or the usual clichés, 'Filadelfia immediately, Champions' League in a few years,' preferring a more measured approach admitting that: "The Filadelfia is sacred and must be restored. However the most important thing now is creating a team capable of escaping from Serie B and claiming our rightful place in Serie A." The name of Marazzina was bounded as the first possible signing.

Cairo's offer though was still to be presented formerly to the Lodisti. He made it clear that any deal would have to be immediate, he wasn't one for waiting or dragging out negotiations. And that he wanted 100% of the club, leaving nothing to the Lodisti nor a consortium of supporters.

Cairo's message was immediately well received by the tifosi, and websites already spoke of a new era and of a saviour. In reality, not everyone was as keen as the mayor and the fans for Cairo's arrival. Marengo maintained that the Lodisti would not give up 100% to the publishing magnet having worked so hard to save the club when nobody else was prepared to do so. "There are still some important things to define," said Marengo, "Remember other significant entrepreneurs like Calleri and Cimminelli have taken over the club and look where we finished."

"We will keep at least 15% for popular action," he continued, "which will act as a umbrella on which the management of the club can be controlled. And not before the 24th August when the club is transformed from a srl to an spa can quotes be sold."

This standoffish stance from the Lodisti annoyed Chiamparino who reminded the group: "If it wasn't for the intervention of Smat as sponsors, the Lodo Petrucci would have remained an illusion and Torino would now be in Serie C2. Cairo has a serious project. An offer like this won't come again for 20 years." Chiamparino left the door ajar for the Lodisti to have some kind of say in the future of the club, saying: "Cairo just needs to guarantee an active role for the Lodisti and not close the door to popular action. I am prepared to act as the mediator between the two parties."

The Cairo interview in *La Stampa* was published on a significant day - the day of the official presentation of the Torino Football Club. At 11:00am at the Bar Norman, the bar which saw the birth of the club, Marengo, Rodda, Giovannone, Padovano and Stringara presented themselves to the press and as many fans as who could squeeze into the venue as possible.

Marengo did most of the talking, recalling what had happened in the summer, praising the supporters, and revealing the extent of the work the Lodisti had already undertaken. He was also noted for his string puppet-like twitches which made him an easy object of ridicule. It seemed the presentation of the new club was an opportunity to articulate the plans of the Lodisti and the extent of the 'popular action'. However, much to everyone's surprise Marengo made a surprise announcement confirming that the Lodisti were prepared to give 100% of the club to Cairo. Padovano and Stringara sat nervously aware that their Torino futures could be over before they started. Giovannone remained stone silent, his presence largely unnoticed.

Marengo's statement put the ball firmly back in Cairo's court. Marengo left Bar Norman in tears to the applause of supporters relieved that he was prepared to make way for Cairo. His reign as Torino President would be a short one and the emotion overcame him. One fan stopped Marengo on his exit from the bar uttering the words, "You should walk out with you head high. You helped save Toro, now give it to Cairo without asking for a euro or a place on the board and you will pass in the story of Torino as a great man."

Meanwhile, the team continued training in Giaveno without kit, training equipment and in a sad sate. On-trial Czech 'keeper Martin Lejsal even turned up in a shirt fit for the beach.

Saturday 20 August

In the morning the newspapers almost unanimously reported the imminent passage of Torino Football Club to Urbano Cairo. "Cairo has his hands on Toro" claimed *Tuttosport*, confirming that Marengo no longer wanted to keep the 15-20% he had initially requested for the Lodisti. Incidentally, the name, Giovannone, appeared in none of the dailies.

Cairo maintained an air of caution: "Don't call me President," he warned, adding: "It's still too early. I still need to see the documents of the club which will be a key moment in determining whether the deal can go through." Marengo met Cairo in Asti, in a meeting which should have confirmed the passage of Torino Football Club to the Alessandra-based entrepreneur. Instead, it marked the beginning of the longest two weeks of the club's history, as the nightmare summer got worse.

RAI's TG3 regional evening news programme revealed that the meeting between Marengo and Cairo in Asti had gone badly. Cairo stated in an interview that it would need a miracle for the situation to resolve itself. The two parties had spent the day in an intense meeting where Marengo's renewed reluctance to give up 100% of the club met Cairo's desire to have complete control, choose his own men, and conclude immediately. The crux of the problem, as well as Marengo's insistence in keeping part of the club for the consortium, lay the responsibilities already untaken by the Lodisti.

Three days earlier when Cairo enquired about buying the club he was told that the Lodisti had signed no contracts and they had just made verbal offers and commitments. When Marengo reached Cairo in Asti it was brought to light that 46 contracts had already been signed - by players, coaching staff and former club employees.

Cairo didn't want to undertake any of these responsibilities, worried that accepting former employees of Cimminelli could be viewed as a continuation of business (the club had been declared dead by the F.A but Cimminelli still owned the Torino Calcio company until a tribunal would declare it officially bankrupt or not. The ex-patron still held possession of the club's former trophies and brand) and that he could end up inheriting some of the club's former troubles. On a footballing front, Stringara and the players signed under Padovano were not wanted by Cairo nor potential Coach Gianni De Biasi, with the Presidential candidate confirming: "We would have only signed three of them."

Marengo and Rodda had betrayed Cairo's trust by going from their 'hand shake' story to turning up with signed contracts, some even signed after Cairo had warned them not to take on any more responsibilities. The publicist magnet was in volcanic mood as the deal seemed to have stalled.

"It's not a question of money," added Rodda. "But of morals and respect for the people with whom we have made agreements and commitments. But we are prepared to pass on the ball."

Sunday 21 August

A day of reflection. The newspapers reported the rift between Cairo and the Lodisti, with the only positive news coming from Chiamparino's message of mediation and belief that the disagreement was as much the two parties pulling the cord as hard as possible in order to get the best deal.

Cairo cooled off enough on the Sunday to agree to a meeting on Monday at the town hall which could have signalled the passage of the club to the publicist.

Monday 22 August

The day began with the promise of heated negotiations but with a potentially pleasant finish. The day Torino got what they wanted after a summer of fear and pain.

Cairo arrived at the city hall ten minutes before 1 o'clock to meet with Paolo Peveraro (responsible for the council's budget), expressing his interest in taking over the Stadio Comunale (now back in the council's hands) and acquiring more advertising space in the Olympic centres. Chiamparino was in Tropea, Calabria for a few days of holiday but was kept abreast of events via telephone. Within an hour Cairo and Peveraro were joined by the Lodisti to begin negotiations to take over the club.

An hour later, Cairo's right-hand man, Trombetta, met with some fans who had gathered in the piazza confirming Cairo's strong intention to buy the club. Soon after, Peveraro revealed that the meeting was going well and that there was a 75% possibility of a possible agreement before the close of play. More fans, having followed the affair via the internet appeared at the municipal.

By 6 o'clock the mood was not quite so serene. Gianni Bellino, vice-President of the Lodisti admitted that there were some serious and unexpected problems, and left the meeting in a state of shock and despair. Within 45 minutes, the problem had a name - Luca Giovannone. The man who had been praised for helping save Torino, the man who had only appeared briefly in newspapers in those stupid phone-in-hand office shots and who looked permanently liked he'd just been punched in the head, was about to change the scene. Giovannone proclaimed that Cairo hadn't bought Torino. He had.

It emerged that a private agreement between the Lodisti had given 51% of the club, and therefore the majority, to Giovannone who with the help of two mystery benefactors from Rome 'had no intention of selling it.' "I will only reveal the names of the financiers," said Giovannone almost threateningly, "when I've given the cheque to the notary and confirm that 51% of the club is mine." The two names banded about were those of Roberto Mezzaroma, a constructioner, who had shares in Lazio and Claudio Lotito, President of Lazio. "We're ready to take Torino back to Serie A," stated Giovannone, who just four days earlier had remained silent in the press conference when Marengo declared his intention to give Cairo 100% of the club. At the time, Giovannone already had his private agreement. Yet, nobody had thought to mention it. Not Giovannone. Not Rodda and not Marengo.

At 19:45, Cairo emerged to speak to the press. "It's a horrible day for me and the Torino supporters," said a crestfallen Cairo. "I discovered after a six hour meeting that 100% of the club which was promised to me was not available. I have been taken for a ride. I was even prepared to agree to all the contracts we had discussed."

Marengo and Rodda were left red-faced admitting that were they resigning from the club and apologised to Cairo and the fans. Marengo had found himself hopelessly out of depth and whether through incompetence or malice, he had put the new club in a precarious position and nobody was quite sure why. Had Marengo given Giovannone the majority share of the club to preserve his own interests, having understood that with Cairo in charge he would be ousted? Whatever his motives, innocent or not, he hadn't counted on Cairo's popularity with the tifosi.

Cairo, in turn, came out to speak to the 200 or so supporters who were in the piazza, myself included, where we would spend most of the next ten days. "I was ready to buy the club," he confirmed. "The meeting went well in the afternoon, I was even prepared to accept certain conditions and lies. Then Giovannone walked in and said he owned 51% of the club and didn't want to sell it. He had a private agreement signed by Rodda and Marengo." Cairo ashen-faced and visibly tired, maintained a sense of dignity above everything and was applauded as it took him half-an-hour to reach his car parked in the piazza. 'Non Mollare Mai - Don't give up,' 'Non Mollare Mai,' chanted the tifosi as Cairo left to a hero's reception but to a sea of doubt, admitting that it may be October or November before he could move again to buy the club.

Cairo poignantly added: "It is clear that someone recently said that Turin was too small for two teams and it seems someone is trying to stop me buying the club." As Cairo's car pulled out towards via Garibaldi, it seemed the last hope of peace and a bright future passed with it.

That evening a group of ultras stormed off to Giaveno to speak to the players and asked them to boycott the club and this new character, Luca Giovannone.

Tuesday 23 August

"Torino still in caos" reported *La Stampa* the next morning as Turin woke to a sea of questions. 'Giovannone tiene il Toro - Giovannone holds onto Toro' reported *Tuttosport*. 'In the morning Torino were Marengo's, in the afternoon virtually Cairo's, and by the evening Giovannone entered the fray.'

Why had Cairo delayed all weekend and not rushed the deal, if he was so keen on concluding immediately? Why had he bickered over a few contracts when if he is so rich he can pay the people off? Did Cairo really want to buy the club? Why had Giovannone suddenly spoke up? Who was behind Giovannone? What are his motives?

Giovannone and his 180,000 euro had helped pay some early bills but he had shown no intention of ultimately running the club nor seemed to have the finances to do so. What's more during the press conference at the Norman days earlier when the Lodisti confirmed that they would give 100% to Cairo he remained silent and this was considered in bad faith. What's more in his press conference on the Monday evening he presented himself badly, stuttering and half finishing sentences.

"I am the real owner and tomorrow I'll prove it in front of a notary," said Giovannone threateningly. "When Cairo pulled out of the race on Saturday, I confirmed to Marengo and Rodda that I had the funds to go the distance. At that time, some important entrepreneurs from Rome called me and offered their support."

Still little was known about this Giovannone character, beyond that he was 41 and had an obsession with Graziani. He graduated at 23 years of age with top marks in psychology (a young age in Italy to graduate) and gained wealth importing foreign nurses, mainly from Eastern Europe to work in hospitals. He seemed in no rush to present himself.

What's more it appeared that the private agreement signed between the Lodisti and Givoannone giving him 51% of the club had been signed after Cairo had appeared on the scene, between the 17th and 19th August, which put the Lodisti in a contentious position. Marengo's standing after Monday night's escapade was already precarious.

Chiamparino was in a volatile mood on his return from holiday admitting that "a little bird from Rome informed me that Lotito is behind Giovannone," and that he felt like he'd been taken for a ride by the Lodisti. The mayor gave Giovannone 24 hours to present what his plans were for Torino FC and reveal who he was working with. Chiamparino also added: "This is a comedy of misunderstandings which risks a tragic finish." If Giovannone didn't articulate his intentions, the mayor would push for Torino to be given to someone capable of taking the club forward, i.e Cairo, after all it was Smat that sponsored the Lodo Petrucci.

That evening at the town hall, Cairo, Giovannone, the Lodisiti and Chiamparino met to discuss the future and possession of the club. The atmosphere outside the city hall was intense. Unfortunately, the August holidays still swelled a large number of tifosi yet around 300 people waited outside the town hall including a number of the organised groups.

Circling the piazza proved a dangerous habit over the next week as different groups predicted/retold/invented what was happening inside. 'The deal is done,' 'Giovannone doesn't want to sell,' 'Marengo has forgotten a document,' 'On Ansa it says that unless by tomorrow night we have an owner we won't play in Serie B.' And so it continued. The only link to the fans waiting outside in the piazza, who filled hours of worry, boredom and anguish by eating kebabs, reading newspapers, playing with mobile phones, were from the five ultras invited into the meeting.

The groups were much more varied than the anti-Cimminelli marches of July. Perhaps a number of the young people were away, a number of ultras certainly were and there were more pockets of people, fathers and daughters, elderly couples, groups of hairy student types, obese people, the trumpet blower, kids skinning up, but few signs of violence to warrant the mass carabinieri presence.

Every couple of hours one of the ultras would exit the meeting and sit on the spiked fence surrounding the monument infront of the city hall and try, without loudspeaker, to tell a couple of hundred impatient people what was going on. The crux was this: Giovannone held 51% of Torino FC but wouldn't, it seemed, be able to deposit the cheque for the club to officially become recognised as a company without the support of Marengo who by now and by default was in Cairo's camp. If Giovannone wasn't prepared to sell to Cairo and wasn't put in a position to take at least temporary control of the club then Torino Calcio risked extinction the next day. If the Lodo Petrucci wasn't ratified then the side would be demoted to the regional leagues or possibly Serie C2. The fans didn't want Giovannone, who had presented himself badly and not revealed what he wanted to do with the club. However, without Giovannone or his goodwill, the club couldn't be passed to Cairo.

The fans began understandably losing their patience, with chants of "Giovannone pezzo di merda – Giovannone piece of shit," "Noi vogliamo Urbano Cairo – We want Urban Cairo," "Giovannone e Lotitio a Torino fate schifo - Giovannone and Lotito you make Turin sick."

By eleven o'clock it seemed a breakthrough had been made. Giovannone agreed to sell the club to Cairo, via a scrappy piece of paper, if he was given between 1% and 49% control of the club but negotiations would continue the following day. It seemed a pass had been made in the right direction. However, a man willing to accept anything between 1% and 49% hardly seemed a sharp business mind.

Wednesday 24 August

The longest day. By midnight the future of Torino FC should be resolved.

Late in the afternoon the negotiating parties met at what was becoming their second home - the town hall. Fans began to wait outside from the late afternoon as frustration grew and rumours spread. One school of thought, and it seemed the most probable one, believed that Giovannone was working on behalf of Lotito, the Lazio President in a bid to create a wastepaper basket for Lazio's garbage.

Before the early 1990s, Lazio were a reasonable size club with a passionate and hard-core right-wing fan base, whose one chink of glory was a Scudetto win in 1974. However, Lazio became a major force in Italian football during the 1990s, thanks to the heavy spending of Gianmarco Calleri - the man who would save and then ruin Torino - and then Sergio Cragnotti of Cirio[16] fame. It was Calleri who in 1992 brought

---

[16] CIRIO is one of Italy's largest food companies, producing primarily tinned products. Former Lazio President Sergio Cragnotti took over the company when it was privatised in 1993.

Paul Gascoigne to Rome, prompting Channel 4's coverage of Italian football, when the league thanks to its monopoly on foreign talent, domination of Europe, financial muscle and well-organised league was a far cry from the regression and disorganisation of today. Lazio under Cragnotti spent, spent and spent and after some cup success finally claimed the league title in 2000 having invested millions of euro on the likes of Christian Vieri, Alen Boksic and Juan Sebastian Veron as well as on overrated coach Sven-Goran Eriksson.

However, in buying themselves the title and regular Champions' League football, Lazio also ate themselves into serious debt and when Cragnotti left the club he may have taken it to its most successful spell in history, but the cancer underneath the surface to ruin. When Lotito took over, Lazio had over 100 million euros of debt but were sensationally given 23 years to spread their debts and pay them off. Something not afforded to Cimminelli's Torino.

Consequently, Lotito has sought to rid Lazio of its Cragnotti high-earners, cut the wage ball and consequently the club's ambitions. It seemed that a way of reducing Lazio's debt could be to offload high earners and some of the club's financial problems to newly formed Torino and drive a club fresh from the coffin back to the graveyard. However, as soon as this rumour was surfacing, Lotito distanced himself from Giovannone claiming that Giovannone was not a friend, nor did he even have his phone number. What's more it transpired that a phone call received by Chiamparino via Giovannone from a man claiming to be Lotito was a hoax.

Rumour two, and a popular one, surfaced around the black and white team in the city. For a long time the 'Turin is too small for two teams' insisters Moggi and Giraudo had not missed a moment to belittle Torino. What's more the potential collapse and troubles of Torino opened up the possibilities for the other team to possibly takeover the Stadio Comunale instead of investing in a brand new Stadio Delle Alpi. Further more and with a long term aim, they sought to gain the big swell in support missing for their team in the city. The black and white side had already started producing pamphlets for the Olympics announcing themselves as "....ntus Torino". Further fuelling the fire was the presence of former Gobbo Padovano, Moggi's friend, who was linked to the Gea - the football agency ran by Alessandro Moggi - son of Luciano and which controlled a number of key players and coaches in Italy. This rumour was less a knee jerk one, more a long-held suspicion.

Another angle was analysing who could profit from Torino's potential fall? Should Torino miss the deadline to convert the Lodo Petrucci into a club, then the team would be expelled from the league and replaced in the second division by Napoli, another one of Italy's great clubs, a club that a number of political institutions wanted back in the big time, and who a year earlier had been declared bankrupt, demoted from Serie B to C1 and had just missed promotion by losing a play-off final. Talk was rife that the 'power' behind Giovannone was from Naples. This claim had a short life span as Napoli's season started three days later and once their season started they wouldn't be able to switch divisions.

The negotiations between Cairo and Giovannone's lawyers proved fraught, the former rereviewing the contracts he'd checked on Monday only to find that additional contracts had been added. Fans outside spoke of new contracts for Lazio players being discovered - another urban myth. What was true was that Padovano couldn't be found when he was needed to respond to various questions regarding the contracts which only he had rectified.

Earlier in the afternoon it seemed a breakthrough had been made with Cairo even stepping briefly onto the balcony to wave to the fans to the chorus of 'Presidente, Presidente'. Cairo managed to relay one message to the fans: "I'm used to completing deals of the heart in the evening even missing the birthday of my daughter. I hope to celebrate two birthdays this evening." The hope was again short-lived as Cairo was called back into the meeting following a new problem.

By 7 o'clock Giovannone and Padovano were nowhere to be found, both telephones were switched off and rumours spoke of Giovannone fleeing to Milan or back to Lazio. Should Giovannone not present himself by midday on Thursday and convert Torino into an spa then the club would not be able to survive. Chiamparino tried to located Giovannone but vainly admitted: "He is a free man and can do what he wants. It's the law." Cairo spent the evening meeting with the Lodisti, lawyers and members of the Turin city council but without the good will of Giovannone nothing could change. With the Lazio rumour gaining credibility, Lotito remarked: "I have no interests in Turin and deny categorically that there are negotiations with Torino. I don't even have the number of Giovannone who says he is my friend to reinforce his position."

There was also some bad feeling in the piazza. The Press were not welcome in the municipal and were forced onto the street with the fans who demanded news and crowded round the group of journalists who sought to make their stories straight. Some fans vented their anger against *La Stampa* for some of their negative stories written during the summer.

The atmosphere in the piazza boiled over, with news from the ultrà groups coming far too seldomly to ease the long moments of boredom. There were also some nasty incidents. A group of girls were robbed by two Moroccan pickpockets infront of the carabinieri who played with phones and smoked cigarettes whilst some **ve fans almost caused a fight by shouting remarks from a passing bus. "La pazienza sta finendo - the patience is wearing thin," chanted the fans. Giovannone insults had replaced those against Cimminelli. The general suspicion was true - Giovannone didn't want to sell, had escaped, becoming the villain for the second time in three days.

At 2am, Cairo and Chiamparino emerged to speak to the fans confirming they would not give-in and ensured that Giovannone would.

Whether Giovannone was bargaining for a better effort or wanted to harm Torino was still unclear. Thursday should open up his motives a little more clearly. Before leaving, Giovannone had revealed to journalists: "I'm in relaxed mood seeing as my lawyers are defeating those of Cairo. I'm sick of the bad feeling against me, which has been ignited by Chiamparino. I will be the President of Torino."

Thursday 25 August

Another decision day. The papers were all united, Cairo the good and Giovannone the evil, none of the dailies able to explain the latter's motives or predict what he would do next. It was the day in which Giovannone was expected to deliver the cheque, which would confirm his ownership of the club. The belief was that if he didn't present himself today, then the club's future could be in gross doubt, due to external pressures, particularly from the Italian Football Federation, that the difficult situation resolve itself.

Naturally, the ultrà groups mobilised to force Giovannone's hand and demonstrate the lack of support for his bid. A full boycott of a Torino FC run by Giovannone was planned. Only Cairo would count. The fans had decided, that whatever happened, today was the day that the situation had to be resolved. It had reached the proverbial boiling point.

It was an amazing day which I followed via the internet, www.carlonesti.it, www.sweb.it, www.toronews.net, all providing a commendable, sometimes not credible (the circle of rumours even confused journalists), minute-by-minute guide to an amazing day.

The fans initially waited at the municipal blocking the tram line before moving to the notary with a blockade of Corso Re Umberto where a couple of hundred tifosi demanded to enter the offices of the notary in the hope of meeting Giovannone. Their efforts were in vein as Giovannone again failed to show-up and his whereabouts remained unclear. Some spoke of him being back in Rome, others in Milan, others that he had even committed suicide.

In the meantime, Chiamparino and Cairo began looking at legal ways of ousting Giovannone. There was talk of the mayor requesting a new Lodo Petrucci, cancelling the old one in the light of such dramatic circumstances, but this was immediately rebuffed by the FA. Or of Cairo bluffing Giovannone's private agreement and Marengo signing off on the original 100% and selling Torino to Cairo but this would have serious legal implications and Cairo never really considered it as a viable option.

Rumours around 2pm surfaced that Giovannone and Padovano had been spotted in the Hotel Campanile in Moncalieri. A BMW with Lega Calcio contracts in the passenger seat had been discovered. Within half an hour, a couple of hundred supporters were outside the hotel, some even entering to try and physically carry Giovannone to the municipal to hand over the club to Cairo. A police barrage arrived in time and the fans were forced to wait outside, although some damage was done with three policemen suffering minor injuries. The car which belonged to Padovano was smashed to bits and violence threatened to blow over. Chiamparino ordered Giovannone to the municipal but the entrepreneur was not prepared to move due to the threat of violence and despite his declaration that: "I am a man of the streets and not scared of anything."

Again Giovannone reeled off a series of bizarre comments adding: "I don't care about a car as I have insurance. I wouldn't be seen dead in a BMW and only drive Ferraris." Padovano in the meantime had managed to find an escape route - by foot. The manager of the hotel protected her daughter, doing so by pretending it was a film. Indeed it seemed like *Dog Day Afternoon*, a drama played out on a stifling afternoon with everybody's patience taken to the limit. The Prefect of Turin Goffredo Sottile even made an emergency return to the city to try and speed up negotiations. But Giovannone would not budge. And the fans wouldn't give an inch.

However, within a few hours a disagreement between some of the ultrà groups broke out about how to handle the situation and Giovannone took the opportunity to escape via a police escort, heading not to the municipal but back to Lazio. Chiamparino had warned that even if a vase of flowers broke the deal would stall, and some fans understood the pacific message of the mayor better than others, who wanted to deliver a more physical message.

Later that evening the groups met in the city but little was possible without the presence of the head of Vita Serena. However, a bright cloud did arrive on the horizon with news after an emergency meeting at Lega Calcio that Torino had until the 9th September, the day before the season started to register themselves for the league and their place was not in threat. The immediate problem was resolved, and Giovannone's non-appearance at the notary to register the club was not yet a problem. However the ownership situation showed no signs of finding any kind of a solution. That night, like Padovano's car, the windows of the ****tus store in via Garibaldi were smashed.

Another sad story came from the ritiro[17] where the team were unable to dispute a simple friendly because they didn't have a kit to wear. Certain

---

[17] The ritiro literally translates as the 'retreat', used in Italian footballing terms when teams lock themselves away from the world, either before big games or during the pre-season.

players were mocked like the African Doudou ordered to go and sell cds and the veteran Brevi told to retire.

Friday 26 August

Giovannone confirmed via the press that he had no desire to sell Torino and would not bow to bullying from Chiamparino nor Cairo nor the violence of supporters. "I want Torino," he proclaimed. "I have some important players at my disposal and I am a legitimate person. I risked my life and for this reason I won't give up." And then rather bizarrely: "I love the ultras and they will learn to love me and soon they will chant Viva Giovannone." By this time he really seemed like Rupert Pupkin from The King of Comedy as Chiamparino and Cairo fought for the Jerry Lewis role.

One of the funniest statements of the summer came from the respected Turin writer Gramellini when talking about Giovannone in La Stampa, 'Turin, its people and political institutions are being held hostage by a man who can't finish sentences who wears suit sizes five times too big.' During the few times he'd spoken to the press, Giovannone proved as graceful and articulate as a drunk in a kebab shop.

Chiamparino announced that his mediation with Giovannone was over due to the latter's habit of changing the cards on the table and added that there would be no political concessions or favours made to Giovannone should he pursue his desire to retain the club with the stadium remaining the property of the council. Cairo was equally frustrated, admitting: "I offered Giovannone 1,8% of the club and a position to take some profits, not any of the potential losses and he refused. I'm being taken for a ride, it's not a negotiation. If Giovannone wants to talk then he should make himself available. If he wants double, triple, quadruple his investment then I'm ready to negotiate." Giovannone was clearly acting in interests of this more powerful party, given his nature of going into hiding to make negotiations and inability to clarify his motives or his economic potential.

One supporter added: "The situation we are living in is surreal, not worthy of a club of our tradition and support. Behind Giovannone there is someone powerful but we are here to defend our faith. Supporting Torino is not only a passion but a way of living." The newspapers confirmed this growing fan power 'I padroni sono gli ultra - the owners are the ultras," wrote *La Gazzetta Dello Sport* following the Hotel Campanile incident.

As *La Stampa* reported that having threatened to boycott and ruin the Winter Olympics during the anti-Cimminelli marches the proposed threat was now ****ntus matches. "If things don't go as we hope," proposed one ultrà, "We will make sure that the Bianconeri don't play their home games next year."

It was also clear that with Giovannone in charge of the club, season ticket sales would be minimal, few people would sign up to any pay television deals and as Chiamparino expressed: "With a person as unreliable as Giovannone the council could never sell the stadium, it could only be rented and at the proper market price." There would be zero support for such a club. A club's potential under a man like Giovannone was weaker than that under Cimminelli.

Friday, however proved to be the calm after the storm, Giovannone lying low, Cairo preparing his next move.

Saturday 27 August

Giovannone's next destination was the hospital. In this surreal drama which didn't promise a conclusion anytime soon (despite the fact that within days Giovannone's option to buy the new club expired) the latest twist emerged. Whilst relaxing on a Lazio beach (the fact that he was able to relax an amazing concept in itself) Giovannone suffered symptoms of a heart-attack and was taken into hospital as a precaution.

Cairo and Chiamparino sent messages of goodwill, adding that health comes first and that Giovannone should think about his young family embroiled in this drama. Torino fans were not so charitable. Had the news been that he had suffered a heart attack, most would have been happier.

Nevertheless, Giovannone had 72 hours in which to deposit the necessary cash to convert Torino into a company. This was the final deadline. If he failed to show, Cairo would then be able to take 100% of the club, also receiving the 49% guaranteed by the now exasperated Lodisti. If Giovannone did show then the club was his, what he then did with it was his choice.

Meanwhile in the morning papers some more soundbites from Giovannone emerged. "I won't sell to Cairo nor deal with him anymore. I will be the Torino President and exert my right to pay the 5.1 million euros necessary. My lawyers are already in touch with Marengo."

"I am prepared to die for Torino," he proclaimed before making an about-turn admitting: "Lotito and Mezzaroma are not my partners," days after confirming they were. More bizarrely: "I love the ultras and they will love me too. Our rapport is getting stronger all the time and when we get promoted, I will be their hero."

In the meantime, famous Torino faces signed a petition against Giovannone from Pulici to Agroppi to Sala to Castellini followed by various actors, politicians and families of former Presidents. On the playing front, Lazio striker Muzzi confirmed he was ready to join Torino whether it be for Cairo or Giovannone and the Siena-bound Marazzina launched an attack via the press admitting, "It's because of Giovannone that I'm not a Torino player. Also, had the Lodisti met with some of us former players they probably would have retained most of the team."

The growing political pressure against Giovannone was not only in fervent in Torino but also in his own home-town of Ceccano and amongst his own An[18] political associations, where Giovannone had aspired to be mayor.

Sunday 28 August

A day of reflection. Giovannone recovered. Cairo waited.

---

[18] The An party translates as the National Alliance - Alleanza Nazionale. It is a right-wing party and its President is the extremist Gianfranco Fini

Meanwhile, even the players enjoyed two days of holiday whilst whoever was running the club, and in theory it was still the Lodisti had to find a hotel to host the players once they regrouped on Tuesday.

An interview with Ciccio Graziani in *Tuttosport* being one of few items of note. Graziani, from the same region as Giovannone and the player who inspired Giovannone to become a Torino supporter, was now a coach for a reality-tv side. Unlike his ex-colleagues, Graziani called for mediation: "If both parties really want Torino and really want the best for the club, then they should stop arguing and find an agreement. With good sense and intelligence it's possible."

Graziani admitted he was flattered by Giovannone's admiration for him. "I'm not on anyone's side," said Graziani. "I've read the petition against Giovannone but won't sign it. Instead of telling him to get lost, I want to tell him to think about it and the eventual consequences."

Giovannone reaffirmed his promise of arriving in Torino on Wednesday with a cheque 'between his teeth'.

Monday 29 August

Serie B had officially started at the weekend but few games were played. Pescara versus Torino naturally didn't go ahead to allow the Granata time to prepare for the new season. Only four games, those in Verona, Catanzaro, Bari and Trieste went ahead. Others didn't due to the protest against the new proposed Serie B kick-off slot of 4pm on a Saturday afternoon which was created to allow the division to find its own nichè in the television market.

The opposition to this proposition not only came from fans but principally from the mayors of the respective cities who, seeing as the council's owned a large part of the stadiums, refused to open them. Reasons ranged from fears for public safety seeing as Saturday afternoon was principally shopping time and several stadiums are located in the centre of towns. Many cities used the areas near the stadium for markets on a Saturday, such places would therefore suffer a potential loss of income. Fans, naturally, preferred an evening kick-off to the afternoon as many worked or had family commitments. Once again, Italian football had let a summer-long issue drag on into the start of the season.

For Torino, these problems were irrelevant, these were now days of waiting as midnight on the 31st August would confirm what Giovannone's intentions were for the club, whether he had the money or whether he had bluffed. If Giovannone did care about Toro, his actions seemed a little strange, seeing as he was pushing the club into a situation where they were about to miss the transfer deadline to sign players and with the season ever closer. *La Stampa* confirmed Giovannone's intention to bring the five Lazio players Manfredini, Inzaghi, Muzzi, Lequi and Robert to the club.

One pleasant notice in this summer of doom came from Florence, where images of Fiorentina supporters holding aloft 'Forza Cairo' and 'Ultras Granata Non Mollare Mai' banners were displayed during Fiorentina's game against Sampdoria as a mark of brotherhood, seeing as Torino and Fiorentina are twinned. The twinning system sees ultras from various clubs unite in pacts of friendship and peace. Torino's principal and loyal friends are Fiorentina and Genoa, and if travelling to see any of these three teams play you will be sure to see shirts and scarves of the other two teams.

Principally, Fiorentina have a long standing rivalry against the 'other team' after League Championships fought and lost and following the sale of Roberto Baggio to the **ve in the early 1990s. Surprisingly the only team in Italy not twinned with anyone are the black and white side, universally hated as they are loved by 12-year old Swiss boys.

Tuttosport continued to lead the campaign against Giovannone and emphasised his link to Lazio. It transpired that he had previously made enquires into buying Atalanta and Venezia and questioned why if he promised to invest so much money into Torino had he only put forward 180 thousand euros.

What's more nobody was able to analyse how many private agreements Giovannone had at his disposal and what the nature of the 51% he had signed via Marengo and Rodda was actually worth legally. What was apparent was that Cairo didn't want to run the risk of 'stealing' the club on the basis of the private agreement not being valid.

Marengo, meanwhile, diverted some of the attention towards the grave situation that within 12 days the team faced their first game of the season, but not without adding his voice against Giovannone, "He has completely betrayed the projects undertaken as a team, taking on his own independent route. I hope the illness he has suffered has given him time to reflect and take a pass back. But my relationship with Giovannone has finished, we now speak via our lawyers."

Marengo admitted that in hindsight it would have been difficult to have taken a different route. "Like it or not, the only one who came forward when Torino needed an investor was Giovannone. It's to easy now to say we would have never opened the door to him."

Tuesday 30 August

'Torino in sala d'attesa - Turin in a waiting room' reported *La Gazzetta Dello Sport* as Giovannone remained at home and no cheque had yet been deposited. Meanwhile, the team returned to training this time in Rivoli and stayed at the Hotel Villa Savoia thanks to the charity of its owner, who offered the club free stay at the hotel.

Torino Cronica sought to get behind the myth of Giovannone at his home town of Ceccano. Little had been revealed about this wannabe Rupert Pupkin. Giovannone it turned out was son of a manual worker, and both his parents unlike him were left-wing, political speaking. Giovannone enjoyed close relationships with men of political importance in the area such as the senator Oreste Tofani and Francesco Storace. He had campaigned to be mayor of Ceccano.

The same paper published an sms received from Giovannone which claimed, 'I am under a specific medical program and undertaking interviews could create problems.' Giovannone also maintained that via his accountant Lorenzo Tiberia he would deposit the money needed to become patron of the club by midnight of the 31st.

One resident of Ceccano raised the point. "What does he want to do in Turin?, why not invest his money here? And he knows nothing about football." They confirmed that Giovannone was a supporter of Milan and not Toro. His main football experience was limited to a spell as patron of Rio Ceccano, a five-a-side female team.

Wednesday 31 August

Nobody was sure whether Wednesday 31st August would provide a final conclusion or an end to this summer of drama. However, Giovannone's intentions for the club would become clearer. He nor an associate still hadn't presented themselves with that famous 'cheque between the teeth', and had until midnight to do so.

Marengo, who had already created enough damage, was prepared to refuse any cheque given by Giovannone but with the obvious judicial implications nobody wanted this affair to drag on yet further. Some members of the An party, of which Giovannone was a member, admitted they were trying to convince him to give up the ghost. But by now, Giovannone knew that after the hell he had created, giving up would see him lose face. Something a man with a psychology degree and a past as patron of a women's five-a-side team could not afford to lose.

It was a day when the Press embarrassingly struggled to follow the story as all parties involved called bluffs. There was a reported sighting of Tiberia, the man with the cheque between his teeth at Turin airport but he never arrived as far as the notary. Reports that Giovannone and Cairo were negotiating inside the town hall surfaced, prompting the familiar faces to meet in the nightly ritual of starring aimlessly at the three flags on he municipal balcony, chase any cars that passed in case Giovannone was passing and able to explain himself, eat kebabs from the nearby takeaway on via Milano, reminisce in a communal depression which was somewhat therapeutic.

What was most striking was the diversity of people who suffered this faith. Elegant Piedmontese women, tamarri, groups of old men who had seen the Filadelfia in its splendour and Mazzola at his peak, young children and families, student types who spent all day on internet sites like Toronews which thanks to the traumatic summer had become one of the top 100 clicked internet sport sites in the world.

Most people spent their time on the telephone speaking to the privileged few who followed the affair via the internet and consequently learnt the bullshit and the truth before we did. However, our presence was a sign of force and support. Torino fans gave great visibility during these months, which were also of great unity.

Not present on this crucial night were the ultrà groups whose voice was so desperately needed. The difference of opinion over the Hotel Campanile affair had led to some tension. Some groups were upset with others that they had let Giovannone escape and the lack of unity between the various ultrà groups had caused fractions. Young boys enjoyed the task of becoming the ultras for the evening, but their voices tame and unthreatening as much as they were credible.

For most of the evening it wasn't apparent if anyone was in the municipal until a few of Cairo's lawyers briefly made themselves visible. At the same time Ansa confirmed Giovannone was the new President of Torino, although other sites diffused this news. Again, moving across the piazza, different groups had different versions of the event.

Only by ten o'clock was the truth a little clearer. Cairo was not in the municipal. Nor was Giovannone. Their sets of lawyers were. No cheque had been deposited. Cairo and Giovannone were in Rome at the Fuminicio Airport bought together apparently by the senator Salerno whose mediation had convinced Giovannone to do exactly that - mediate.

The lack of news circulating the piazza was frustrating. The Tg3 Piedmont news show that had almost dedicated every opening story to the Torino affair for a month reported little of note. Across the day it was revealed that several transfer targets that had understandably not been able to wait any longer for the Giovannone versus Cairo affair to resolve itself. This being the last day of the transfer window.

Consequently players who had given their word to Cairo moved on. Cristiano Doni, an international only a couple of years earlier, transferred to Mallorca in Spain although he even called Cairo after landing in Spain to see if a deal could be resolved at the last minute. Marazzina, in tears, moved to Siena against his will. The experienced Ezio Brevi who could have joined his even more experienced brother Oscar, decided to accept

Catania's more stable future and strengthened a prospective Serie B rival.

But as this affair proved, when the things went quiet, something either bad or good was usually brewing. The atmosphere in the piazza intensified, the hope that the 31st night would be the last of this painful summer. Everyone gave their last drop of energy and conserved their remaining hopes. The long periods of silence and confusion interspersed by reflection and rumours. In the age of the internet and sms, people still gathered in the piazza for news.

At 23.35 it was confirmed that a deal had been signed, Torino belonged to Cairo and Giovannone had relinquished his 51% for 1.8% of the club. A massive step backwards on the part of the latter. The news broke to the tifosi in the piazza prompting a mass celebration and after so many false dawns, promises, last minute hitches and negotiations, the future was the one they had dreamt. Urbano Cairo was the 28th President of Torino Calcio or the 1st of Torino FC.

Why had Giovannone made this dramatic late concession of the club? Had the Lazio plot become too transparent?, and his associates from Rome therefore step backwards? Was he such a bad poker player that his indecision had weakened his bargaining power? Had political pressure squeezed him out and made him think twice about the repercussion for his political future? Had the Napoli plan gone to fruit once the Lega Calcio confirmed Torino would be in Serie B? Had he realised that should he take control of Torino he had no support, even had his intentions been genuine, seeing as no fan would watch the team under him, nor any Piedmontese company deal with him? Did he realise finally that he was out of his depth and the 'man of streets' could not handle anything more than a women's five-a-side team? Had the heartache as minor as it had been made him reflect on life? Had Rupert Pupkin simply enjoyed his 15 minutes of fame?

Giovannone's official reply was this: "I have the money and my project was serious. I had Milanese, Piedmontese and Roman businessmen behind me but I won't reveal their names. However, I suffered threats and fears for my family, and the threats to them and not to me where the problem. Once the threats were to my dears (his wife and three children) and my 600 employees, I said enough. Those delinquents who threatened me won."

"Chiamparino didn't understand me," added Giovannone (who could understand a deep man of such baffling intelligence), the ambiguity of Rodda and Marengo caused problems and certain phrases could have been avoided. When it was said that should Torino finish in the hands of Giovannone it was the end of the club, it made me feel bad."

In the months to come Giovannone relinquished the right to the 1.8% he was said to possess. He had left without anything. His parting note was a strangely positive one. "Cairo is an excellent entrepreneur and knows how to succeed. I will continue to support Torino like I have done since the times of Graziani."

So what of Cairo? Probably a good night's sleep was in order after concluding an affair which he had virtually concluded twice and which after some early doubts he wanted to complete to the bitter end. The overriding sensation was one of relief. The future could wait at least 24 hours.

But Torino fans could rest assured that the most respectable face had been confirmed as President since Sergio Rossi after the trash of the last twenty years. Finally after Presidents who bludgeoned the club for money, after men who had sold the club's dignity, after years of depression and after the pain of Cimminelli and Romero, Torino had a real President.

Chapter 9 – The Resurrection

'Cairo straordinari per il Toro - Cairo's extraordinary efforts for Torino' read the headline of *La Gazzetta Dello Sport* which a day after the long, final night of Cairo against Giovannone, jumped straight into the future with their article on the new owner. "It was a shame I couldn't have been in the piazza to celebrate," admitted Cairo. "They tell me the celebrations were something else." Indeed they were.

Cairo spoke of his pride at completing a deal which seemed finished twice and then seemingly dead in the water. The publicist again emphasised the support of his parents whose passion for the club grew out of watching the Superga orphans lose 7-1 at Milan, and their passion eventually drove him to complete one of the most complicated of football takeover bids.

"Buying a football club is never a deal," admitted Cairo. "My choice was one from the heart due to the passion of my parents. What was the reason I entered the frame so late? Because the Lodisti seemed to be working well and didn't need external help. Only when I heard Chiamparino worried did I start to think and concentrate myself on a deal."

Building a football team and a club in a little over a week is a thankless and nigh on impossible task but that was the scale of a problem facing Cairo following his 11th hour deal to sign Torino Calcio. The club paralysed by the Giovannone affair still had nothing bar contracts for thirteen players, most of whom were unwanted by the new club.

Although their contracts would be honoured, their Torino futures were over before they started.

These footballers had trained with minimal equipment under trying conditions. Several training sessions had been cancelled. They hadn't played a proper friendly and worked under a shadow of doubt and under a Coach - Stringara - who was destined for the sack once Cairo appeared on the scene. "Time is against us" admitted Cairo. "We have already lost important players and those who have remained need to be remotivated."

"When you take over a new company," continued Cairo, "You need to immerse yourself, at least in the beginning, into every tiny detail to see how it operates. However, the work will not only be difficult but enjoyable as well." For the tifosi, Cairo was handed automatic hero status, immediately earning the nickname Papa Urbano - a reference to Urbano being a common Papal name.

In an interview with *La Stampa* he confirmed his desire to reintroduce a high quality youth team. "The youth system is fundamental and needs to be nurtured with care. It is important for the young people of the region but also the economic future of the club. Torino will create young players who know how to play the right way."

Cairo had already located the club's new headquarters above Cafè Zunigo on via Roma, taking the club back into the city centre and in a prestigious area of the city. The move was only temporary as with the move to the Stadio Comunale a year later the club were hoping to lay down their roots at the newly-constructed stadium. Cairo was unstoppable in these first few days, bound on by a positive energy and a release after his victory over Giovannone, who had already slipped into the 'infamous for fifteen minute' archive.

Cairo immediately put one of his designers in charge of developing the club's new logo, which was to be a throwback of the large, powerful bull from the 1970s inside the outline of the Scudetto shield. Wishful thinking can't hurt, while eliminating the association with the city of Torino and complemented with a brand new Asics kit with the correct shade of granata after the plum reddy shirts of the Cimminelli era. Immediately popular with the tifosi.

"Liberati da un incubo - Liberated from a nightmare" read *Tuttosport's* headline. "Il Toro and its supporters have finally found some peace," whilst reporting also not forgetting the pale state of the team who the day earlier had played a match against the youth side in a kit not fit for a school team.

Tuttosport did something they rarely do - promote Torino to the front pages of their newspaper, relegating the 'other team' to page six. They even ran an extended welcome letter from Cairo under the headline 'Facciamo Il Torino - Let's make Torino'. Cairo underlined his intention to follow the path already led by President Pianelli using him as an example and a model, emphasising his desire to "promise little and deliver a lot." "I don't intend on eluding nor betraying supporters as has occurred in recent years," continued Cairo.

"We will aim to reach Serie A," vowed the new President, "I want for calm and patience but am also a very ambitious man and slowly, slowly want to create an extremely ambitious Torino that will be financially secure and victorious on the field." Cairo impressed both the fans and the media, his delivery that of a man polished in the communication field.

"I thank the fans, Chiamparino, the assessor Peveraro, my lawyers and their teams," continued Cairo. "I also thank Galliani, President of the Lega Calcio, who stayed close to me, a help which was not only moral." Papers spoke of a return of Zaccarelli even as eventual President, or of Luciano Nizzola, former head of the Football Federation, but Cairo was keen to press that no negotiations had taken place with either man.

The team were even able to train in something semi-official for the remainder of the week as De Biasi began to coach a team which had not played a serious friendly, had not trained properly, had never played together before and was still desperately short of quality and quantity. Nevertheless De Biasi called upon "aggression and good football just like Chelsea," adding: 'We may be defeated on the field but not with out heart and pride.'

Cairo was officially confirmed President two days after becoming so, for the records pen met paper on the 2nd September 2005 and he presented De Biasi to the Press and the fans whilst holding aloft a portrait of the 1949 heroes. The Coach confirmed he had turned down major offers to come to the club although not all were convinced.

The Coach in Italy has a different role in respect to a manager in other countries. He usually has no say in player transfers, who comes and who goes, will find various directors interfering in team policy and his job expectancy is short. The Coach is there to coach, inherit a style of play, train the players (although he has a bulk of staff for this as well), pick the team and deal with the Press, which in Italy, must be about the most trying part of the job.

Cairo's promise of nine quality new players was his first lie. Ten arrived, despite the club only being able to sign players unwanted by their employers or free agents. The first official signing of the new Torino was Enrico Fantini, signed on loan from Fiorentina. A Gobbo youth product, Fantini's career had never reached the heights it should have done but at the age of 29 now was something of a final opportunity. His main physical characteristics being his bald head and sticky out ears, making him something of an Italian Billy Whizz.

After Fantini arrived veteran 'keeper Massimo Taibi. The former Atalanta player is best remembered for two nightmare spells at Milan and Manchester United, where he failed even to catch a cold. However, when playing in the provinces he had always excelled as a quality 'keeper. The move was a surprising one considering Toro already had Pagotto and Fontana available.

The following signings were hardly of the quality of what was expected but they were welcome never the less. Defender Giovanni Orfei had spent the last few years in the Serie B basement with Venezia and Salernitana and had hardly been a regular at both. Nevertheless he knew De Biasi from his successful days at Modena and like Fantini, Luca Ungari and Vedin Music, a player curiously never booked in his career in Italy, were reunited with the 49-year old boss.

Davide Nicola, Turin born and bred, but never a Torino player joined the club he supported as a boy, but in his thirties added Serie B experience rather than long-term quality. Surprise, surprise another Modena player completed the defence line-up with Jacopo Balestri, fresh from three years in Serie A replacing BalzaGobbo as left-back and at the prime of his career came with the reputation for actually being able to cross a ball.

The principal midfield addition seeing as Ardito, Gentile and Vailatti had already been recruited was Mark Edusei, signed on loan from

Sampdoria. The Ghanaian midfielder had spent the best part of a decade in Italy and would face the task of replacing Mudingayi in the team's engine room. A surprise move saw U-21 international Alessandro Rosina recruited from Parma, a player who could play both out wide or through the middle, with pace to sell and some delightful touches. In essence the fantasista needed to replace Pinga.

On the final day available for transfers Raffaele Longo was recruited from Roma, a player whose career had taken a severe nosedive after a promising start and sought a resurrection under the Mole. The attack remained the area most in need of reconstruction with only youngsters De Sousa and Bongiovanni secured under the Lodisti offering meagre options. The promise was for a '20-goal a season' striker. Options included the mega-earner Marco Di Vaio of Valencia, although this seemed to be a thought provoked by the drunken optimism of some Toro fans, Massimo Maccarone of Middlesbrough whose shaven head would fit in with those of Brevi, Rosina and Fantini and Antonio Langella of Cagliari who had fled from the club's training base into exile after a disagreement with a group of ultras he called 'imbeciles'.

In the end it was a bald player who would spearhead the frontline. Roberto Stellone had passed a somewhat curious summer. He began it promoted to Serie A with Genoa for whom he scored 17 goals to help secure the Rossoblu a top-flight place. However, like Toro, Genoa were not to enjoy their newly found top division status but for a different motive.

Having dominated most of Serie B, Genoa stuttered in the closing months of the campaign but still seemed in control of a promotion spot. A team which had been constructed at a high cost were in danger of deluding patron Enrico Preziosi, owner of a large and successful toy company. Genoa's future centered around a match against Venezia, won 3-2 at home on the final day of the season. Venezia were pathetic, without most of their first team and already relegated.

The Venetians actually gave the game a surprising sense of life, leading by a goal for most of the first half and equalising in the second period. However, days after the game it was revealed that a Venezia director had left the Marassi stadium in Genoa with a suitcase with 250,000 euros inside. It transpired that the money was from Preziosi and ensuing court cases failed to clear his name or buy the excuse that the payment was for Venezia player Ruben Maldonado. The payment it seemed was for the match.

Consequently, Genoa were relegated to Serie C1, shot to bits and lost several of the big name players they had already signed for Serie A. Venezia, incidentally, also went bankrupt and started again from Serie C2.

Stellone began to look for pastures new. He had at one point left Genoa for Lazio but the deal stalled. Then he looked certain to move to Messina but days later it revealed he hadn't actually signed. Then he was close to Cagliari but couldn't agree personal terms. In the end Cairo persuaded both Genoa to sell the player and Stellone to stay in Serie B.

Another hot deal was one for Muzzi, a player targeted by Giovannone, who emerged as the principal candidate as second striker. Muzzi's demand of a three-year deal was not appeased and he eventually settled for two, the 34-year old Serie A veteran signing 45 seconds before the transfer window closed due to the stubborn resistance of the Lazio patron, him again, Lotito.

Muzzi arrived at Torino hours before the season opener against Albinoleffe but still managed to take his place on the bench, probably introducing himself to his team-mates in the meantime. The positive energy and relief leading up to the first game of the campaign was palpable, it seemed like Christmas had arrived after months of depression.

The problems associated with a new club forming had their effects. Without a proper headquarters or office, tickets were difficult to obtain and only at the 11th hour was an agreement reached to make them available in certain tobacconists across the city and outside the ground on the day of the match. What's more, a new law in Italy required that all tickets be personalised which further confused the bureaucratic procedure in a country where bureaucracy rules in all the wrong places.

The Pisanu law was introduced in July 2005 as a way of identifying who enters stadiums in order to crackdown on violence in the stadiums. However, in a country where it is ridiculously easy to break into grounds due to a massive police presence not realising that a day at the stadium is not a cigarette break, where there is no video surveillance inside nor outside the ground, where a large number of stadiums - particularly in

Serie B - are dilapidated and look like throwbacks to the 1970s, where there is no presence or stewarding of curvas, crowd control or what is taken into stadiums, it seemed a space age measure in light of the other problems.

30,000 people did buy tickets for the game against Albinoleffe, although some of the ultrà groups had not put to bed their Hotel Campanile disagreement and consequently, the first game of the campaign passed by without banners, flares or drums. Those who did show up made a good noise. Cairo Americanised the moment taking his young family under the curva to a rousing reception, such an ovation for a President in Italy, about as unlikely as a tabloid journalist attending a rock star's birthday party.

The opponents brought few fans, in reality Albinoleffe being one of the smallest teams ever to play at the level of Serie B. Merged from the two towns - Albino and surprisingly enough Leffe - they were the amalgamation of two smaller sides and in the late 1990s enjoyed a rise through the ranks up to Serie B. Hailing from the Bergamo region, they are something of an Italian MK Dons[19] with a heart. Indeed, Albinoleffe remain the only visiting team to have visited the museum dedicated to Il Grande Torino.

De Biasi's starting XI for the first game of the campaign saw eleven debutants, something that had not happened to a Torino team since the Superga disaster. Only Vailatti who was introduced as a second-half substitute featured from last year's squad. Immediately, the new Torino impressed as a fresh, young tigerish bull and they took the lead early in the match. Balestri's cross after 16 minutes was met by the head of Fantini whose effort despite protestations was adjudged to have the crossed the line. The old Torino would have probably not been given the goal.

The team controlled the game, playing some tidy football and with a pacy, lively attack spearheaded by Stellone and the neat footwork of Rosina, who was only denied a debut goal by the post. The victory proved more than the fans honestly expected but following a summer of torment, hate, passion, love, ridicule, comedy, politics, seiges, protests,

---

[19] MK Dons play in the English professional leagues created as a kind of franchise when Wimbledon Football Club were relocated to Milton Keynes.

marches, transfers and unparalled drama it probably wasn't so crazy after all.

"Il Toro è rinato: vicente - Toro are reborn: winning" reported *Tuttosport* which applauded the application and spirit of the new team as well as the big turnout from the public. Even the usually conservative *La Gazzetta Dello Sport* was excited, announcing: "Questo Torino va dritto al cuore - This Torino goes straight to the heart" and in a secondary article: "Cairo e la Maratona: è già amore - Cairo and the Maratona: it's already love."

Days later Cairo, thumbs up in a suit jacket, but with the new Torino shirt tucked underneath, spearheaded the photo shot for the new season-ticket campaign which prompted another police presence outside a random, otherwise tranquil street in Turin. This time the fight was on for one of those precious season tickets and eventually almost 20,000 were sold - the highest figure in 14 years, only a few thousand shy of the most supported team in Italy™, who had practically given away up to 5,000 of those season tickets for the equivalent of one euro a game and who for the first few league and Champions' League football matches of the campaign, commanded lower crowds than Toro in B.

Cairo appeared everywhere as a positive, progressive and ambitious figure. Torino became fashionable again with features in just about every magazine, newspaper and television program and a RAI two-part film on Il Grande Torino, which beat Harry Potter in the ratings chart. Within weeks Cairo had reinstalled in the club what had been missing for a decade. Torino's glorious history was never more fervently celebrated, its future had never looked more promising.

Epilogue - The Future

Torino fans don't want Champions' League football (although it would be nice) nor a Scudetto immediately. They ask to be respected, for the club's traditions to be maintained and for an ambitious debt-free future. What was certain was that is was better to face Serie B, Albinoleffe and Cairo than Serie A, Milan and Cimminelli on the 9th September 2005.

Cimminelli retained possession the trophies and trademark of the former club and refused in a final pathetic act to let them go until a tribunal ruled in November 2005 that his Torino were finally bankrupt, and he no longer held possession over anything. The former honours went up for auction.

The disastrous Cimminelli, though, is not the sole culprit of the death of Torino Calcio. The rot started with the debts accumulated later under the two-faced Borsano. Respective Presidents Goveani and Vidulich were naive in affronting the challenge only immersing the club in further debt. Calleri managed to save the club front the brink of bankruptcy in the summer of 1994 but at the amazing cost of cutting the club down to the bones, a position it was never able to recover from.

Cimminelli was as naive as he was arrogant. He employed the wrong people in key positions and let the club's debt roll whilst becoming a shining example of the arrogance of modern football where debts are allowed to accumulate at no expense. Romero proved a tragic appointment, Mazzola a nostalgic mistake, and Cimminelli's rapport with coaches, players and above all the supporters were never short of terrible.

Without a Russian millionaire or a strategic Keynes-style economic recovery plan, Torino probably would have gone to the wall sooner rather than later. The errors of Fiorentina and Napoli proved more than poignant warnings. However, it wasn't only the financial problems under the Cimminellian era that are left as a legacy of the Torino that died, but the complete lack of respect, pride and dignity which reigned during his tenure presiding over the club.

Even the new club flirted with death. The Lodisti may have had honourable intentions but were out of their depth with the scale of the task they faced and the mayor knew it. Chiamparino's work in August should be commended, first finding the sponsorship to guarantee the Lodo Petrucci and then finding Cairo, a man capable of offering the club a new start. The mayor worked hard as a mediator throughout the summer, and he was not only motivated by the desire to resolve a major problem a year before the Olympics took place - he is a Torino fan as well.

The Lodo Petrucci enabled Torino to reform at a dignified level, not the fourth division which faced Fiorentina a few years earlier. However, the new club were placed in inexperienced hands and the bumbling Giovannone was given the power to ruin the club without anyone researching who he was, what his potential was and what his vision for the club was. Even months after his exit, nobody can confirm whether his intentions were good or evil.

The ex-players, on the whole, protested in the light of the Cairo deal that they would have stayed at the club and the Lodisti did too little to convince them to stay. However, few hung around to give even the Lodisti enough time to offer deals. Poignantly, none had made an impression in the early months of the Serie A campaign. Mantovani, Marchese, Mudingayi, Keller and Balzaretti had barely played, Pinga performed badly at Treviso and only Quagliarella and Comotto played regularly. They had been so obsessed with playing in the top-flight but potentially taken a step backwards by doing so. They watched on as the new Torino made an impressive start to the Serie B campaign, in a bid to regain promotion.

The role of Chiamparino, the Lodisti and Cairo was paramount in salvation and then resurrection of the club. However, the only group to remain united during the summer of shame were the club's supporters, who having already witnessed drama of all sorts, watched despairingly as a Shakespearian-type tragedy was played in front of their eyes, by villains indifferent to its conclusion. Under the years of Cimminelli, the fans found new unity, their own ways of honouring the past and recreating a spirit in the club. Under Cairo, they have a President capable of leading them and creating enthusiasm.

Within hours of becoming President, Cairo had already done more good for the club than Cimminelli. His battle against Giovannone, when the club's supporters really had already seen to much, will probably only enhance his standing, Cairo emerging as a William Wallace style hero against Giovannone, the wasted years under Cimminelli and the powers, whoever they were, that wanted to kill the new club before it had been baptised.

Cairo's reign may or may not bring success. Only time will tell. He is not a billionaire but he has the intelligence and expertise to spend the significant amount of money he is willing to invest wisely. He is lucky to inherit a club with no debts, where supporters are desperate for a saviour and for whom a new stadium, and all of its financial advantages, in the heart of the city is constructed. He is shrewd enough to ride on the quest of the positive wave, but also to maintain his promises. He is humble enough to ask for advice, aware of his inexperience in the football world.

Torino supporters have a heart and have a story which has made their existence so special. There is always room for sentimentality. Cairo must find the balance between preserving the club's tradition and roots but using them to modernise a club which could dominate Italy and who knows flirt with Europe as well.

The playoff final victory against Perugia wasn't entirely wasted and revenge could eventually be enjoyed. In a bizarre sense, the play-off for a place in Serie A was essentially a play-off to avoid Seric C. Meanwhile, Cimminelli's sidekick, Romero, is still on Ergom's payroll and is probably still promising that his boss will deliver that bank loan.

More importantly, the enthusiasm recreated by Cairo helped Torino fans participate in the Winter Olympics with pride and fervour. In many of the venues, Granata supporters were visible with banners and scarves on display. The Look of the Games adopted in the city was a red close enough to Torino's Granata shirts. The video feature played before the daily Medals Ceremonies and concert at Piazza Castello ran a goal by Toro's Alessandro Rosina and not **ve's Alex Del Piero. The colossal American television network NBC produced a feature on the rise and fall of Torino, and interest in the club was at an all time high. The motto of the Olympics read 'Passion Lives Here'. It was an inspired slogan.